Simple Chinese Astrology

DAMIAN SHARP

Conari Press

This paperback edition first published in 2006 by
Red Wheel/Weiser LLC
With offices at:
500 Third Street, Suite 230
San Francisco, CA 94107
www.redwheelweiser.com

Book design: Claudia Smelser
Cover design: Donna Linden
Cover, text calligraphy, and illustrations: Lei Yang

ISBN-10: 1-57324-261-6
ISBN-13: 978-1-57324-261-5

LIBRARY OF CONGRESS CATALOGING-IN-PUBLICATION DATA
Sharp, Damian
   Simple chinese astrology / Damian Sharp.
      p.   cm. — (A simple wisdom book series)
   Includes bibliographical references.
   ISBN: 1–57324–261–6
   1. Astrology, Chinese I. Title II. Series
bf1714.c5 s44 2000
133.5'9251—dc21   99–045033

Printed in the United States of America
MV

10 9 8 7 6 5 4 3 2 1

SIMPLE CHINESE ASTROLOGY

FOREWORD

Of course in reality there is no such thing as "Simple" Chinese Astrology. Chinese Astrology is a complex, mystifying, and difficult philosophy. But, as Damian Sharp so capably demonstrates in his handsome book on the subject, Chinese Astrology can be *made* simple. We can all grasp its basic meaning and perhaps even learn how to make use of its lessons in our daily lives. What it comes down to is this: The year in which you were born not only defines your character, it seals your destiny.

The truth is, whether you're a fair-minded Dog or a feisty Dragon, a nomadic Tiger, or a laid back Snake, your animal sign is vitally meaningful. A flinty Rooster does not behave in the same manner as a stolid Ox. And independent Horses don't get along with relentless Rats for long without coming to blows. The problem-solving Monkey and the elegant Rabbit don't hit it off in bed and the Goat is the genius *artiste* who happily depends on outside forces for his security. The Pig? He or she likes authenticity—and money.

In this compact book, Damian Sharp describes each animal sign in detail and shows how one of the five Chinese elements will affect a person's character. He also gives us insights about what it means to have been born in one hour or another as well as how we will fare in all of the twelve years to come.

Chinese Astrology might not be simple, but in this concise and handsome volume Damian Sharp has aptly shown just how easy it can be to understand the basics.

Suzanne White, 2006
www.suzannewhite.com

THE FASCINATING WORLD
OF CHINESE ASTROLOGY

When Westerners ask, "What's your sign?" they are almost invariably referring to the system of Western astrology that tracks the influence of the planets and stars on human personality. But there is another ancient system of astrology that is not as well known in the West—Chinese astrology. We hear about it, if at all, in newspaper articles referring to Chinese New Year (occurring around the end of January and the beginning of February). We hear that this year perhaps is the Year of the Rabbit, or of the Dragon. But there is a whole, complex horoscope system behind these words, a system that can unlock mysteries of the human personality and current events in an extremely accurate and uncanny way.

Based on the Chinese lunar calendar, Chinese astrology is a highly poetic system of interpreting both human nature and events. It is not dogmatic or rigid in any sense; it points out the basic characteristics and elements that define our personalities and behavior as well as the time and place in which we live, and it can lead us to a greater understanding of ourselves and of humanity in general. It also enables us to realize our weaknesses in a nonjudgmental way and maximize our strengths, while showing us with whom we can best get along and teaching us how to live and work with others.

While the Communists in China have tried to stamp out belief in Chinese horoscopes, the system, like Feng Shui and Chi Gong, has been preserved in China itself. It has also been greatly adhered to and advanced by overseas Chinese, in Hong Kong, Taiwan, Singapore, Malaysia, the United States, and other areas of the Chinese Diaspora, where the ancient beliefs have been preserved for their practical wisdom.

Once you become familiar with Chinese astrology, you will be amazed by how accurate it can be when you apply it to yourself and the people you know. In China, it is not only considered an ancient and exacting science but an art form as well. What is presented here is a very basic introduction to Chinese astrology that can be applied not only to people, but also to countries, giving us elemental insight into national attitudes and character. It is no mere historical or political coincidence, for instance, that the United States, born in the Year of the Fire Monkey (1776), and the former Soviet Union, born in the Year of the Fire Snake (1917), were involved in a prolonged "Cold War" that was based on nervous mistrust and covert activities, each spying on the other and trying to catch their opponent unaware; or that the American Monkey should at times experience communication barriers with the People's Republic of China, which was born in the year of the stubborn, authoritarian, traditional, and rigid Earth Ox (1949).

WHAT'S YOUR SIGN?

The Chinese horoscope is based on the Chinese lunar calendar, which is made up of five cycles of twelve years each, with a complete cycle taking sixty years. It was introduced by the legendary emperor Huang Ti, known as the Yellow Emperor, between 2700 and 2600 B.C.E. According to legend, Buddha summoned all the animals to come to him before he departed the Earth. Only twelve came to pay their respects, and to honor them in return he named a year after each animal in the order that they appeared, thus establishing the twelve-year cycle: Rat, Ox, Tiger, Rabbit, Dragon, Snake, Horse, Sheep, Monkey, Rooster, Dog, and Boar.

The Vietnamese honor the Rabbit as the Cat, but no Chinese source identifies the fourth animal of the zodiac as the Cat. According to one story, when Buddha summoned the animals, the Cat was to be among them, but the Rat failed to deliver the message and appeared in the Cat's place. Another version has it that the Rat delivered the message, but the Cat was sleeping and didn't want to move. Yet another story states that the Cat was excluded because it had caught the mouse sacred to Maya, Sakyamuni's mother.

According to a Chinese saying, one of these animal signs is "the animal hidden in your heart," and determines the distinguishing characteristics of your personality, behavior, and proclivities according to the year and time of day you were born.

But there is much more to the system. Each of the twelve animals also corresponds to a direction and a season. Also, each sign is allotted one of the five elements of Chinese alchemy (known as its "fixed" element): Wood, ruled by the planet Jupiter; Fire, ruled by Mars; Earth, ruled by Saturn; Metal, ruled by Venus; and Water, ruled by Mercury. The five elements are further divided into positive and negative poles, known in Chinese as Yin and Yang. Yin is feminine, darkness, death. Yang is masculine, light, life. In Chinese art, medicine, and philosophy, everything is classified under these two polarities, which are represented by the *T'ai chi*, the circle divided into Yin and Yang, the dark and the light, the symbol of the origins of all life, the "great primal beginning" of all that exists.

The fixed element ascribed to each of the Moon signs governs it as a whole and affects the sign's basic attributes—for example, the Monkey, whose fixed element is Metal. However, besides the fixed element, a second element is ascribed to each year, and it is the combination of these two elements that define the makeup of any given personality (along with the sign ruling the time of birth). The year 1968, for example, was the Year of the Earth Monkey,

T'ai chi,
the circle divided
into Yin and Yang

while the Monkey's fixed element is Metal. Thus each Monkey will have certain distinguishing characteristics based on the element ascribed to the year of its birth.

The following chart lists the twelve signs and their *fixed* element, season, direction, and polarity or stem (positive or negative). Earth, because it is symbolically composed of all of the other four elements (as well as representing China, "the central kingdom"), is not present in this chart.

Animal	Element	Season	Direction	Polarity
Rat	Water	Winter	North	+
Ox	Water	Winter	North	-
Tiger	Wood	Spring	East	+
Rabbit	Wood	Spring	East	-
Dragon	Wood	Spring	East	+
Snake	Fire	Summer	South	-
Horse	Fire	Summer	South	+
Sheep	Fire	Summer	South	-
Monkey	Metal	Autumn	West	+
Rooster	Metal	Autumn	West	-
Dog	Metal	Autumn	West	+
Boar	Water	Winter	North	-

The twelve animal signs also correspond with a month in the lunar calendar, and therefore can be directly matched with the signs of the Western zodiac (although your Chinese astrological sign comes from the lunar *year* you were born in, not the month).

The Rat, belonging to the month of December, finds its counterpart in the zodiac sign Sagittarius. The Ox in January equates with Capricorn. The Tiger, ruling February, shares many of the characteristics we associate with Aquarius. The Rabbit and Pisces belong to March. The Dragon and Aries cohabitate in April. The Snake and Taurus are associated with May. The Horse and Gemini reside in June. The Sheep and Cancer are akin to July. The Monkey and Leo reign in August. The Rooster and Virgo govern September. The Dog and Libra are linked with October. The Boar and Scorpio come together in November.

In China, certain years are dreaded because of the combination of their element and sign. An outstanding example of this is the Year of the Fire Horse. Women, in particular (an old Confucian bias), who are born in this year are said to wreak havoc on their families and spouses because of their unbridled passions, and in times past a female unfortunate enough to be born in this year might actually be killed as an infant.

The lunar calendar day begins at 11 P.M., and the twenty-four hours of the day are divided into twelve two-hour segments, each ruled by one of the animal signs. Thus the hours between 11 P.M. and 1 A.M. are ruled by the Rat, 1 A.M. to 3 A.M. by the Ox, and so on. As in Western astrology, the sign ruling your time of birth is the ascendant and has a strong influence on your personality. A Dragon born in the Hours of the Sheep is likely to be more modest and diplomatic than we might usually expect from this proud, egotistical, eccentric, and aristocratic animal sign. A courageous and determined Sheep, on the other hand, was more than likely born during the Hours of the Dragon.

The twelve signs are also divided into active and passive, or positive and negative—not in any pejorative sense, but in terms of Yin and Yang (the male and female energy the Chinese believe is the governing force in the universe). The Rat, Tiger, Dragon, Horse, Monkey, and Dog belong to the positive stem, while the Ox, Rabbit, Snake, Sheep, Rooster, and Boar belong to the negative.

GETTING ALONG WITH OTHERS

Chinese astrology provides much information about which signs make good partners, lovers, and friends. Just as with the polarities of a magnetic field, where two positives make a negative, Yin will attract Yang but repel another Yin, as Yang will attract Yin but repel another Yang. Order and harmony in the universe, as well as within the body, is based on keeping the Yin and Yang in delicate balance. In the Chinese horoscope, all conflicting signs belong to the same stem. However, only those signs that are *directly opposite* one another generate any repelling force. When you look at the Triangles of Affinity, you will see how three positive or negative signs can actually be harmonious together when they are 120 degrees apart. A Dragon-Monkey match, for instance, is deemed a highly compatible and beneficial union, even though they both belong to the positive stem.

In the Chinese horoscope, each of the twelve lunar signs is assigned a compass point. Signs that form a triangle make the best unions.

The first triangle is made up of the positive doers—the Rat, Dragon, and Monkey. These are the self-motivated initiators and innovators, full of dynamic energy and ambition, who act without hesitation or doubt. They pair up well with one another in any combination, as they all complement each other's ways of

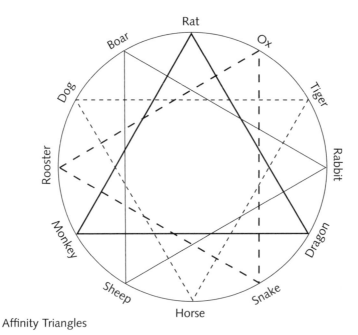

Affinity Triangles

thinking and operating. As we have already seen, the United States of America was born in the Year of the Monkey (1776). The Commonwealth of Australia was born in the Year of the Rat (1900), and these two countries not only share much in common but continue to enjoy ongoing friendly relations. It was the United States, not Britain, that came to Australia's aid during World War II.

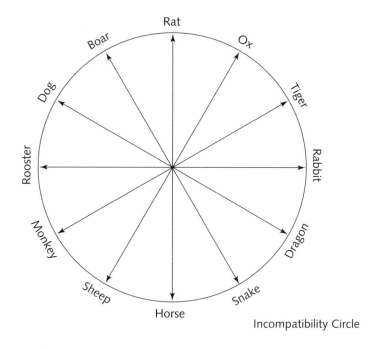

Incompatibility Circle

The second triangle is that of the dutiful and steadfast Ox, Snake, and Rooster. All three are distinguished by their sublimity, constancy, and perseverance. Stalwart and fixed in their views, they are slow and steady in their movements, rely on their own judgments, and plan their actions systematically. Guided by their heads rather than their hearts, they are considered the most intellectual of the signs and like to act independently.

The third triangle is made up of the Tiger, the Horse, and the Dog. They are honest, open, humanitarian, and idealistic. They are social animals, extroverted, energetic, communicative, generous, impulsive, and defiant in the face of adversity and injustice.

The fourth triangle is composed of the intuitive and emotionally driven signs of the Rabbit, the Sheep, and the Boar. These three are expressive and eloquent in aesthetic and artistic ways and rely on their senses and feelings to guide and motivate them. They are thought to be of calmer and gentler disposition and have more compassionate and sensitive natures than the other signs of the cycle. They are drawn toward beauty and the higher aspects of love and advocate peaceful coexistence.

Signs directly opposite each other, as shown in the Incompatibility Circle, are in direct conflict, and any matches between them do not bode well for the long term.

Thus the Rat and the Horse will encounter their greatest rivalries and conflicts with each other, as will the Ox and the Sheep, the Tiger and the Monkey, the Rabbit and the Rooster, the Dragon and the Dog, and the Snake and the Boar.

Signs not directly opposite one another will experience compatibility or indifference to varying degrees, some making very good and complementary secondary matches outside the three primary matches of the Affinity Triangle, for example, a Dragon and a Snake. Incompatibility is based on six degrees of separation.

HOW THE FIVE ELEMENTS
INFLUENCE PERSONALITY

Metal

Those born in years controlled by Metal are ambitious, success-oriented, determined, and persevering. Resolute and unhesitating in conduct and expression, they are guided by powerful feelings, and at times can be unreasonably stubborn and inflexible. They have strong financial acumen (Metal is the element associated with money) and will use it to enhance their appetite for luxury and power. Willful and opinionated, they need to learn the value of compromise and desist from rigidly insisting on always having things entirely on their own terms.

Water

People born in years ruled by Water are fluid, like their element. They penetrate rather than dominate, and like a river or stream, are able to wear away any obstacles in their path through their quiet and indomitable perseverance. They are skillful communicators, able to transmit their ideas and influence others. In their negative state they can be too conciliatory and passive, and over-reliant on the support of others. To succeed, they must learn to be more assertive and actively use their powers of persuasion to turn their dreams and visions into reality.

Wood

Those born under the Wood element are said to possess high moral standards and advocate consistent growth and renewal. They are extremely self-confident and progressive, with executive abilities that enable them to take on large and cooperative ventures. Because of their generosity and innate and sympathetic understanding of others, they are able to generate support and financial backing for whatever they undertake. Their main drawback is an enthusiastic and overconfident tendency to take on too much and thus risk accomplishing nothing.

Fire

People born under the influence of this element are natural-born leaders, charismatic and dynamic in speech and action. Adventurous, ambitious, impulsive, and undaunted by risk, they have the greatest capacity to inspire others and realize their goals. Their forcefulness and ambition, however, can also work against them, and they can become selfish, inconsiderate, and restless when unable to get what they want. The warmth and brightness of the Fire element naturally draws people to them, but it can also be destructive when not kept under control.

Earth

Those born under the Earth element are known for their pragmatic and conservative natures. They are prudent with their finances and are capable planners and administrators. Reliable and methodical, they are not given to exaggeration or embellishment, and can be expected to present things simply as they are, or at least as they see them. On the negative side, they can suffer from a certain lack of imagination and adventurousness, and can be too critical and overly concerned with protecting their own interests.

USING THIS BOOK

To go further, you need to find your sign by referring to the table on the following pages which details the lunar years for each sign.

To use the system as a fortune telling device, you can read the first section of each sign—it details the general characteristics of a particular year that are applicable for everyone. For instance, the year 2000 is the Year of the Dragon. By reading what the year will be like, you will gain insights into general forces and tendencies.

Sign	Lunar Year	Element
Rat	January 31, 1900 to February 18, 1901	Metal (+)
Ox	February 19, 1901 to February 7, 1902	Metal (-)
Tiger	February 8, 1902 to January 28, 1903	Water (+)
Rabbit	January 29, 1903 to February15, 1904	Water (-)
Dragon	February 16, 1904 to February 3, 1905	Wood (+)
Snake	February 4, 1905 to January 24, 1906	Wood (-)
Horse	January 25, 1906 to February 12, 1907	Fire (+)
Sheep	February 13, 1907 to February 1, 1908	Fire (-)
Monkey	February 2, 1908 to January 21, 1909	Earth (+)
Rooster	January 22, 1909 to February 9, 1910	Earth (-)
Dog	February 10, 1910 to January 29, 1911	Metal (+)
Boar	January 30, 1911 to February 17, 1912	Metal (-)
Rat	February 18, 1912 to February 5, 1913	Water(+)
Ox	February 6, 1913 to January 25, 1914	Water (-)
Tiger	January 26, 1914 to February 13, 1915	Wood (+)
Rabbit	February 14, 1915 to February 2, 1916	Wood (-)
Dragon	February 3, 1916 to January 22, 1917	Fire (+)
Snake	January 23, 1917 to February 10, 1918	Fire (-)
Horse	February 11, 1918 to January 31, 1919	Earth (+)
Sheep	February 1, 1919 to February 19, 1920	Earth (-)
Monkey	February 20, 1920 to February 7, 1921	Metal (+)
Rooster	February 8, 1921 to January 27, 1922	Metal (-)
Dog	January 28, 1922 to February 15, 1923	Water (+)
Boar	February 16, 1923 to February 4, 1924	Water (-)

Sign	Lunar Year	Element
Rat	February 5, 1924 to January 24, 1925	Wood (+)
Ox	January 25, 1925 to February 12, 1926	Wood (-)
Tiger	February 13, 1926 to February 1, 1927	Fire (+)
Rabbit	February 2, 1927 to January 22, 1928	Fire (-)
Dragon	January 23, 1928 to February 9, 1929	Earth (+)
Snake	February 10, 1929 to January 29, 1930	Earth (-)
Horse	January 30, 1930 to February 16, 1931	Metal (+)
Sheep	February 17, 1931 to February 5, 1932	Metal (-)
Monkey	February 6, 1932 to January 25, 1933	Water (+)
Rooster	January 26, 1933 to February 13, 1934	Water (-)
Dog	February 14, 1934 to February 3, 1935	Wood (+)
Boar	February 4, 1935 to January 23, 1935	Wood (-)
Rat	January 24, 1936 to February 10, 1937	Fire (+)
Ox	February 11, 1937 to January 30, 1938	Fire (-)
Tiger	January 31, 1938 to February 18, 1939	Earth (+)
Rabbit	February 19, 1939 to February 7, 1940	Earth (-)
Dragon	February 8, 1949 to January 26, 1941	Metal (+)
Snake	January 27, 1941 to February 14, 1942	Metal (-)
Horse	February 15, 1942 to February 4, 1943	Water (+)
Sheep	February 5, 1943 to January 24, 1944	Water (-)
Monkey	January 25, 1944 to February 12, 1945	Wood (+)
Rooster	February 13, 1945 to February 1, 1946	Wood (-)
Dog	February 2, 1946 to January 21, 1947	Fire (+)
Boar	January 22, 1947 to February 9, 1948	Fire (-)

Sign	Lunar Year	Element
Rat	February 10, 1948 to January 28, 1949	Earth (+)
Ox	January 29, 1949 to February 16, 1950	Earth (-)
Tiger	February 17, 1950 to February 5, 1951	Metal (+)
Rabbit	February 6, 1951 to January 26, 1952	Metal (-)
Dragon	January 27, 1952 to February 13, 1953	Water (+)
Snake	February 14, 1953 to February 2, 1954	Water (-)
Horse	February 3, 1954 to January 23, 1955	Wood (+)
Sheep	January 24, 1955 to February 11, 1956	Wood (-)
Monkey	February 12, 1956 to January 30, 1957	Fire (+)
Rooster	January 31, !957 to February 17, 1958	Fire (-)
Dog	February 18, 1958 to February 7, 1959	Earth (+)
Boar	February 8, 1959 to January 27, 1960	Earth (-)
Rat	January 28, 1960 to February 14, 1961	Metal (+)
Ox	February 15, 1961 to February 4, 1962	Metal (-)
Tiger	February 5, 1962 to January 24, 1963	Water (+)
Rabbit	January 25, 1963 to February 12, 1964	Water (-)
Dragon	February 13, 1964 to February 1, 1965	Wood (+)
Snake	February 2, 1965 to January 20, 1966	Wood (-)
Horse	January 21, 1966 to February 8, 1967	Fire (+)
Sheep	February 9, 1967 to January 29, 1968	Fire (-)
Monkey	January 30, 1968 to February 16, 1969	Earth (+)
Rooster	February 17, 1969 to February 5, 1970	Earth (-)
Dog	February 6, 1970 to January 26, 1971	Metal (+)
Boar	January 27, 1971 to February 15, 1972	Metal (-)

Sign	Lunar Year	Element
Rat	February 16, 1972 to February 2, 1973	Water (+)
Ox	February 3, 1973 to January 22, 1974	Water (-)
Tiger	January 23, 1974 to February 10, 1975	Wood (+)
Rabbit	February 11, 1975 to January 30, 1976	Wood (-)
Dragon	January 31, 1976 to February 17, 1977	Fire (+)
Snake	February 18, 1977 to February 6, 1978	Fire (-)
Horse	February 7, 1978 to January 27, 1979	Earth (+)
Sheep	January 28, 1979 to February 15, 1980	Earth (-)
Monkey	February 16, 1980 to February 4 1981	Metal (+)
Rooster	February 5, 1981 to January 24, 1982	Metal (-)
Dog	January 25, 1982 to February 12, 1983	Water (+)
Boar	February 13, 1983 to February 1, 1984	Water (-)
Rat	February 2, 1984 to February 19, 1985	Wood (+)
Ox	February 20, 1985 to February 8, 1986	Wood (-)
Tiger	February 9, 1986 to January 28, 1987	Fire (+)
Rabbit	January 29, 1987 to February 16, 1988	Fire (-)
Dragon	February 17, 1988 to February 5, 1989	Earth (+)
Snake	February 6, 1989 to January 26, 1990	Earth (-)
Horse	January 27, 1990 to February 14, 1991	Metal (+)
Sheep	February 15, 1991 to February 3, 1992	Metal (-)
Monkey	February 4, 1992 to January 22, 1993	Water (+)
Rooster	January 23, 1993 to February 9, 1994	Water (-)
Dog	February 10, 1994 to January 30, 1995	Wood (+)
Boar	January 31, 1995 to February 18, 1996	Wood (-)

Sign	Lunar Year	Element
Rat	February 19, 1996 to February 6, 1997	Fire (+)
Ox	February 7, 1997 to January 27, 1998	Fire (-)
Tiger	January 28, 1998 to February 15, 1999	Earth (+)
Rabbit	February 16, 1999 to February 4, 2000	Earth (-)
Dragon	February 5, 2000 to January 23, 2001	Metal (+)
Snake	January 24, 2001 to February 11, 2002	Metal (-)
Horse	February 12, 2002 to January 31, 2003	Water (+)
Sheep	February 1, 2003 to January 21, 2004	Water (-)
Monkey	January 22, 2004 to February 8, 2005	Wood (+)
Rooster	February 9, 2005 to January 28, 2006	Wood (-)
Dog	January 29, 2006 to February 17, 2007	Fire (+)
Boar	February 18, 2007 to February 6, 2008	Fire (-)

Taken from the Chinese Ten Thousand Years Lunar Calendar.

one

THE RAT

Chinese Name: Shu
Direction: North
Fixed Element: Water
Stem: Positive
Western Sign: Sagittarius
Color: Reddish-brown
Flower: Daisy
Fragrance: Sandalwood
Tree: Oak
Birthstone: Emerald
Lucky Number: 11
Years: 1948, 1960, 1972, 1984, 1996, 2009, 2021

THE YEAR OF THE RAT

A year of opportunity and great bounty, in which fortunes can easily be made. A time to make long-term investments. Ventures begun this year will be successful; however, it is important to avoid taking unnecessary chances or risks. Success this year depends on being prudent and discriminating; then all will go well.

THE RAT PERSONALITY

Rats are known to be hard-working and thrifty, shrewd and very adroit at handling and hanging on to their money. Alert and level-headed, they are gifted with foresight, keen intuition, and fine business acumen that is matched equally by their instinct for self-preservation. The Rat's craftiness is proverbial in China, and they always check out the terrain, marking the possible dangers and escape routes, before entering into any deal or transaction.

Although tight with their money, Rats are genuinely caring souls who do not take their relationships lightly. They are true sentimentalists who cherish their families, friends, and associates, and are prone to get entangled in others' affairs because of their strong emotional attachments. Although quiet and reserved on the surface, they are actually easily agitated and full of nervous energy, which they are able to contain, since they are not lacking in self-control. What irritates them the most is idleness and waste of time and resources, as waste in any form is contrary to their own industrious natures.

Rats are highly adaptable survivors with an innate sense of danger. They are also adept at recognizing and seizing opportunity, with little or no reservations about using confidential information or taking advantage of another's weaknesses or mistakes. They perform very well under pressure, and are often at their best when faced with a crisis.

Theirs is a charming, bright, outgoing, and highly sociable personality. They have a forthright and honest manner and enjoy parties and large gatherings. They have a remarkable eye for detail, an excellent memory, and are highly inquisitive and very good at gathering information from and about others, although they are expert guardians of their own secrets. Rats are said to make fine detectives and writers. Raymond Chandler, William Shakespeare, Leo Tolstoy, Charlotte Brontë, Jules Verne, Truman Capote, and James Baldwin all were born in the Year of the Rat.

The female Rat will be a paragon of thrift and frugality, forever recycling old clothes, making meals from leftovers, and stretching the family budget. However, as a mother, she finds it virtually impossible to deny her children anything. Rats of both sexes are superb homemakers and doting parents.

The time of day in which he or she is born plays a vital role in the Rat's life. A Rat born in the night will lead a more hectic life (the night being the time of rodent activity and feeding) than one born during the calm hours of daylight.

When negative, Rats can be terrible gossips and busybodies. Their greatest pitfalls will be their avarice and ambition, wanting too much too soon.

The Rat will be primarily attracted to people of the Dragon and Monkey years. Equally compatible with the Rat are people born in the years of the Ox and the Snake, as well as those born in the years of the Tiger, Dog, Boar, or Rat. Rats will come into conflict with those born in the Year of the Horse, and should avoid marrying a Rooster. A marriage with a Sheep is also ill advised.

Rat children will talk early and have very charming dispositions. He or she is very affectionate and loving, likes to eat, and loves group activities. They reveal their calculating natures very early in life. With other children, they are either nurturing or dominating. It will also be very hard to cheat them out of getting their fair share—if not the biggest portion—of the pie. They are extremely possessive of parents and friends, and can be prone to jealousy when they feel they are not being given enough attention. Rat children are avid readers, and demonstrate an uncommon precocity with the written and spoken word.

THE FIVE TYPES OF RATS

Metal Rat—1960

These are intensely emotional and idealistic Rats, although not as romantic as Rats of other elements. Vivid in speech and action, they advance themselves by moving among the rich and power-ful. They love drama and can be both sensualists and moralists at the same time. Like all Rats, they love money but will not hoard it, as they know they can always make more. They are wise investors and most likely athletically inclined.

Water Rat—1912, 1972

These Rats are very traditional and conservative in their out-look and behavior. They have excellent insight and are skilled communicators, but may not be discriminating about whom they talk to. They are, on the other hand, calculating and shrewd, and know how to please those in a position to aid and advance them. They are very concerned with the acquisition of knowledge and higher education, and will be adept at express-ing themselves via the written word.

Wood Rat—1924, 1984

Progressive and executive types of Rat who know what they want and how to get it. Security is important to them, as are their principles. Good communicators, they exude self-confidence and practical know-how and readily find support for their ventures.

Fire Rat—1936, 1996

Generous and adventurous types of Rat who are dynamic in their outlook and given to the performance of gallant and altruistic acts. Energetic and idealistic, they are independent and very competitive and do not like to feel constricted. They follow the dictates of their hearts, and their fortunes can be mercurial if they are too impulsive or impatient.

Earth Rat—1948, 2008

These practical and realistic types of Rat will mature early and are very thorough in their work. Happiness and contentment are found in order, discipline, security, and purpose. They are very concerned with their reputations and public standing. They base their actions on the tried and true, rarely taking any chances, as a result of which their fortunes increase slowly but steadily. On the negative side, they can be prone to stinginess.

INFLUENCE OF TIME OF BIRTH

The Hours of the Rat—11 P.M. to 1 A.M.

A combination that makes for a "pure" sign—a double Rat. A good writer with a charming personality who may also be somewhat egotistical.

The Hours of the Ox—1 A.M. to 3 A.M.

A very serious and plodding and cautious Rat who nonetheless still possesses the Rat's charm and appeal.

The Hours of the Tiger—3 A.M. to 5 A.M.

An aggressive overachiever who may have an imperious manner. The generous and restless Tiger will be in constant conflict with the Rat's thrifty ways.

The Hours of the Rabbit—5 A.M. to 7 A.M.

An astute, watchful, calculating, mild-mannered, and soft-spoken Rat who will be difficult to get around or defeat.

The Hours of the Dragon—7 A.M. to 9 A.M.

The Dragon's willful determination combined with the Rat's talent for making money will make this individual very successful in business. He or she will be expansive and generous, sometimes excessively so.

The Hours of the Snake—9 A.M. to 11 A.M.

A sly and charming Rat, with all of the Snake's quiet allure, sex appeal, and instinct for hidden dangers.

The Hours of the Horse—11 A.M. to 1 P.M.

A more daring Rat. The Horse's capriciousness may cause him or her to lead a dramatic and turbulent life in business as well as in love.

The Hours of the Sheep—1 P.M. to 3 P.M.

This combination is prone to be sentimental. Both signs are brilliant opportunists and expert at currying favors from those in power.

The Hours of the Monkey—3 P.M. to 5 P.M.

A less sentimental Rat with a brilliant sense of humor. An extremely enterprising combination of acute business acumen and wiliness.

The Hours of the Rooster—5 P.M. to 7 P.M.

Very intelligent and capable, but prone to be vainglorious.

The Hours of the Dog—7 P.M. to 9 P.M.

The Rat's need to accumulate wealth is in direct opposition to the Dog's humanitarian desire for openness and fair-mindedness. However, this combination can produce a writer who is a keen and authoritative social critic.

The Hours of the Boar—9 P.M. to 11 P.M.

A Rat who is greatly inhibited by the Boar's moral reluctance to take advantage of every opportunity.

The Year of the Boar—2007

Excessive demands are made on the Rat's time and money, and business progress is slow. Illnesses could develop complications, and there is the possibility of the loss of money or belongings. A time for the Rat to be on guard and consolidate.

The Year of the Rat—2008

Naturally, a very prosperous year, that will be marked by promotions, achievement, and unexpected gains.

The Year of the Ox—2009

A year filled with more than the usual burdens and responsibilities, but there are indirect benefits gleaned from the good fortune of others.

The Year of the Tiger—2010

Not a good year for any speculative venture. The Rat may be forced to act against better judgment, and there is the possibility of the loss of a family member or close associate.

The Year of the Rabbit—2011

Although this is a calm and quiet year, the Rat must be careful with money. He or she will make new contacts in business, and there is the possibility of adding new members to the family.

The Year of the Dragon—2012

A most auspicious year for the Rat, with excellent prospects in both business and romance.

The Year of the Snake—2013

Illness or financial loss could cast a pall over the first half of this year, but the Rat's luck will return as the year draws to a close.

The Year of the Horse—2014

This is a difficult year, as the Horse stands in direct opposition to the Rat. The Rat could become entangled in lawsuits or be forced into debt if he or she is not careful, and their love lives could also suffer.

The Year of the Sheep—2015

Opportunities present themselves to the Rat this year. The Rat is able to realize some financial success or career gains, although these will involve a certain degree of change or upheaval if they are to be implemented.

The Year of the Monkey—2016

A good year with no serious troubles. The Rat should assiduously refrain from breaking any friendships or partnerships in the Monkey year, as the future repercussions will prove unavoidable.

The Year of the Rooster—2017

All sorts of celebrations are in store for the Rat this year—new partnerships, marriage, business success. A hectic but very good year in which Rats must be careful to avoid injury, as they will be distracted by their busy schedules.

The Year of the Dog—2018

Bad luck comes in threes this year, and the Rat may be unable to act in any way to influence the outcome.

SOME FAMOUS RATS

Louis Armstrong, Lauren Bacall, James Baldwin, Marlon Brando, Charlotte Brontë, Truman Capote, Jimmy Carter, Raymond Chandler, Prince Charles, Maurice Chevalier, Aaron Copland, Doris Day, Gerard Depardieu, Richard Dreyfuss, Keir Dullea, Albert Finney, Jane Fonda, Clarke Gable, Dennis Hopper, Pope John Paul II, Philip Kaufman, Gene Kelly, Machiko Kyo, T. E. Lawrence (Lawrence of Arabia), Henry Mancini, Lee Marvin, Harpo Marx, Thom Mount, Wolfgang Amadeus Mozart, Sidney Poitier, Jackson Pollock, Juliette Prowse, Yves St. Laurent, George Sand, Rod Serling, William Shakespeare, Leo Tolstoy, Spencer Tracy, Jules Verne.

two

THE OX

Chinese Name: Niú
Direction: North-Northeast
Fixed Element: Water
Stem: Negative
Western Sign: Capricorn
Color: Dark blue
Flower: Chrysanthemum
Fragrance: Shalimar
Tree: Pear
Flavor: Sweet
Birthstone: Lapis lazuli
Lucky number: 1
Years of the Ox: 1949, 1961, 1973, 1985, 1997, 2009, 2021

THE YEAR OF THE OX

A year in which success can only be achieved through diligence and conscientious effort, while politics and diplomacy are treated with indifference at best. The conservative Ox favors discipline and traditional ways. Conflicts can arise as a result of miscommunication and inflexibility or stubbornness. Gains will be made this year, but only through conventional methods and not without hard work.

THE OX PERSONALITY

A person born in the Year of the Ox will be calm, reliable, and patient. While they are often stubborn and biased, they are also resolute and fearless. They are traditional and methodical and adhere to fixed patterns of thought and behavior. This makes them appear predictable and unimaginative. The sturdy and dutiful Oxen do not rely on luck or guile. Their accomplishments are all the result of sheer tenacity and plodding and systematic determination. They possess a quiet dignity and a strong moral sense, and are generally respected and liked for their honesty, rectitude, and lack of pretension. They are super-self-reliant, loath to ask others for help, and never resort to unfair means to attain their goals. They build things to last, including their families, and will work diligently to ensure the continued survival and prosperity of their offspring. As providers and heads of their households, their word is law, and they will not tolerate insolence or rebellion, although they are extremely proud of their families and care for them a great deal. The government of the People's Republic of China was established in 1949, the

Year of the Earth Ox. Since then China has progressed slowly and steadily through hard work and dedication to her people, while at the same time dissidence, questioning, and protest have been met with authoritarian intolerance. Mao Tse-tung, a Snake, achieved victory in the Year of the Ox; Ox and Snake are found together in the Triangle of Affinity.

An Ox born during the day will be more aggressive and active than one born at night, while a winter Ox will have a harder life than one born in the summer.

Oxen have strong constitutions and are rarely sick. They are proud and uncompromising and disdainful of weakness. When negative, they can lack compassion and be unapproachable, rigid, and narrow-minded.

Oxen can be naive and awkward in matters of the heart. Their practical, down-to-earth nature has little sense of the refinements of romance and seduction, and they cannot fully understand the snares and enticements of love. Because of their traditional ways, both Ox men and women will insist on long courtships. Both are slow to open up and reveal their true feelings, but once committed they are steadfast and responsible.

Ox women, like all Oxen, are practical, no-nonsense types who run their households according to a strict regimen and see to it that all tasks are performed thoroughly and dutifully. They may not be particularly demonstrative with their affections, but they make ideal partners: honest, reliable, and hardworking.

Oxen have long and detailed memories and can nurture grievances for many years. A wounded Ox can become sullen and morose, and one who has suffered disappointment in love may become a brooding and solitary soul and withdraw into his or her work as a defense against ever being hurt again. On the other hand, they will insist on always settling their accounts. No debts will be left unpaid or favors unrewarded. There will be no great verbal displays—words mean little to the practical Ox; it's action that counts.

Because of their legendary patience, Oxen are slow to anger, but when they do get angry, watch out. They are charging bulls—or buffalo—impossible to reckon with or withstand. Do not try to be a matador; you'll only get gored. Simply keep out of their way until they have calmed down.

The resplendent and flamboyant Rooster makes the best mate for the Ox, filling their lives with color and light. They both have a high regard for authority, efficiency, and duty. The serene and prudent Snake and the indefatigable and sympathetic Rat make equally good partners, and love the Ox for his or her sturdiness and reliability. Another Ox, Rabbit, Dragon, Horse, Monkey, and Boar will also be compatible. An Ox will experience bitter clashes with the rebellious Tiger and the fickle Sheep, and the Dog may find them dull, slow, humorless, and set in their ways.

Ox children are characteristically stoic and tough. They are inclined to talk late, use physical means to settle their arguments, and be adamant about the preservation of their privacy. These children welcome discipline and fixed routines, which gives them a much-needed sense of security. Having a taciturn and serious nature, they do not readily show their feelings, nor are they inclined to joke around. They are extremely naive about the ways of the world and in this regard require the advice and protection of their elders. They have remarkable patience and perseverance, and are reliable and responsible.

THE FIVE TYPES OF OXEN

Metal Ox—1901, 1961, 2021

These Oxen are of few words, but they are capable of being clear and eloquent in expressing what they want. They are very intense, resolute, and determined, and will have strong clashes of will with anyone who disagrees with their views or stands in their way. Obsessed with achieving their goals, they can be aggressive and arrogant. Failure of any sort is anathema to them. People of extraordinary stamina, they can work day and night, and require little sleep. They are not very affectionate by nature and could have scholastic or artistic inclinations. They are very responsible and can be relied upon to keep their word. When negative, they can be extremely stubborn, narrow-minded, and vengeful.

Water Ox—1913, 1973

These are a more flexible and open-minded type of Oxen, although still conservative in their outlook. Shrewd and astute and driven by relentless ambition, they can concentrate on more than one goal at a time and work well with others. Water Oxen will calmly and patiently bide their time, waiting out the opposition as they quietly and methodically work at wearing them down.

Wood Ox—1925, 1985

These are less rigid and more considerate, fair-minded, and impartial Oxen who also possess many of the social graces lacking in the Oxen of other elements. Although still prone to conservatism, they are open to and can even embrace new and progressive ideas. They can react with more alacrity than others of this sign, and this, combined with their steadfastness and openness, can make them capable of amassing great wealth and achieving prominence. They understand the importance of co-existence and teamwork.

Fire Ox—1937, 1997

These combustible bovines are drawn to power and prestige. Fire enhances both the Ox's temper and desire for control. Blinded by their innate sense of superiority, they have a tendency to overestimate their own abilities and eliminate anyone or anything they deem as inappropriate or useless without properly assessing their true worth. They can be harsh, outspoken, and inconsiderate, although they are at heart fair and honest. Forceful and proud, they are capable of waging total war against their foes.

Earth Ox—1949, 2009

The slowest but the surest of all the Oxen. Practical and hardworking, they seek security and stability and will endure hardship and suffering without complaint to achieve their aims. Stolid and persevering, they will stand firm and refuse to relinquish any ground gained.

INFLUENCE OF TIME OF BIRTH

The Hours of the Rat—11 P.M. to 1 A.M.

These Oxen are imbued with the Rat's sentiment and charm. They will be more talkative than most and have the Rat's ability to hoard money.

The Hours of the Ox—1 A.M. to 3 A.M.

A "pure" Ox—stolid, dedicated, self-controlled, slow, conservative, obstinate, regimented, and disciplined. Distinctly lacking imagination and a sense of humor.

The Hours of the Tiger—3 A.M. to 5 A.M.

The Tiger gives this Ox a more lively and engaging personality. The combination of these two fierce animal signs can also make for a volatile temper.

The Hours of the Rabbit—5 A.M. to 7 A.M.

This is a discreet and genteel type of Ox, with more refined tastes and lacking the Ox's usual proclivity for strenuous work.

The Hours of the Dragon—7 A.M. to 9 A.M.

A combination of immense strength, power, and ambition that can be opinionated and implacable.

The Hours of the Snake—9 A.M. to 11 A.M.

Both signs are extremely secretive, and the Snake's influence could imbue this individual with a cunning streak not usually associated with the straightforward Ox.

The Hours of the Horse—11 A.M. to 1 P.M.

A lively and happy Ox—like Ferdinand the Bull, who loved to sniff the flowers. The capricious and restless Horse will make this Ox less steadfast and reliable.

The Hours of the Sheep—1 P.M. to 3 P.M.

A tender Ox, possibly with an artistic side and lenient attitudes. He or she is business-minded, receptive to others, and knows how to use their talents to make money.

The Hours of the Monkey—3 P.M. to 5 P.M.

An astute, sly, and jovial Ox, who may even have a wry sense of humor and a dazzling smile. No problem will be too great for this Ox to overcome, and neither will he or she take their problems too seriously.

The Hours of the Rooster—5 P.M. to 7 P.M.

Dutiful but colorful, these Oxen are prone to argument and the use of rhetoric to achieve their goals.

The Hours of the Dog—7 P.M. to 9 P.M.

A stern moralist, possibly with a puritanical streak that is at least alleviated by the Dog's desire for fair-mindedness.

The Hours of the Boar—9 P.M. to 11 P.M.

Although conservative and demanding, this is a more affectionate Ox whose hard-working tendencies will be matched by the Boar's sensual nature and love of good food.

THE OX'S PROSPECTS IN COMING YEARS

The Year of the Boar—2007

A busy but mixed year, in which Oxen may experience some problems in both work and family life. These troubles, though, are actually minor, and on the whole Oxen fare quite well.

The Year of the Rat—2008

This is a lucky and prosperous year for the Ox, and they will have much to celebrate.

The Year of the Ox—2009

A good year for marriage or the formation of new partnerships, although the Ox's plans may suffer some unexpected delays. Problems are small, but may involve some unwanted travel or entertaining.

The Year of the Tiger—2010

A difficult year, in which the Ox meets with opposition from many quarters. A year to be patient and persevering and not take unnecessary risks or drastic action.

The Year of the Rabbit—2011

Progress is steady this year, although there may be sad news concerning a friend or family member.

The Year of the Dragon—2012

A year marked by many changes and unexpected troubles. Oxen will have to work hard but will be able to further themselves through the help of influential people.

The Year of the Snake—2013

A very good year, in which Oxen are bound to make money and enjoy themselves, although they must be alert to the possibility of betrayal and avoid any misunderstandings with their associates.

The Year of the Horse—2014

A difficult year, in which Oxen may experience unhappiness in love or financial setbacks. Illness due to stress could also greatly hinder their progress, and they could be prone to accidents. Their troubles will start to ease with the advent of autumn.

The Year of the Sheep—2015

A slow year. No illness or quarrels bother the Oxen, although they must be careful as there is the possibility of loss where they had expected gain.

The Year of the Monkey—2016

A lucky year with the potential for prosperous new ventures and partnerships.

The Year of the Rooster—2017

Success and happiness continue, although the Ox must be on guard against being swindled and must not be thrown off balance by some strange or unexpected occurrence.

The Year of the Dog—2018

The Ox's paths are cleared of obstacles. Any problems that do arise are actually smaller than they at first appear. However, the Ox may be forced to travel and experience separation from a loved one.

SOME FAMOUS OXEN

Willy Brandt, Harry Bridges, Richard Burton, Charlie Chaplin, Joan Chen, Gary Cooper, Tom Courtenay, Sammy Davis, Jr., Walt Disney, Gerald Ford, Abel Gance, Adolf Hitler, Emperor Hirohito, Dustin Hoffman, Sir Anthony Hopkins, Rock Hudson, Alan Ladd, Hedy Lamarr, Burt Lancaster, Vivien Leigh, Claude Lelouch, Patricia Neal, Jawaharlal Nehru, Paul Newman, Richard Nixon, Sam Peckinpah, Tyrone Power, Robert Redford, Vanessa Redgrave, Sir Ralph Richardson, Peter Sellers, Rod Steiger, Lee Strasberg, Margaret Thatcher, Vincent van Gogh, Gore Vidal.

three

THE TIGER

Chinese Name: Laohu
Direction: East-Northeast
Fixed Element: Wood
Stem: Positive
Western Sign: Aquarius
Color: Red
Flower: Carnation
Fragrance: Jasmine
Tree: Sycamore
Birthstone: Ruby
Lucky Number: 7

Years of the Tiger: 1950, 1962, 1974, 1986, 1998, 2010, 2022

THE YEAR OF THE TIGER

A tumultuous and volatile year, often one of conflict, disaster, and even war (the First World War erupted in the Year of the Tiger). It is also a time of boldness in which nothing is done quietly or on a small scale. Good and bad are taken to their extremes, and people act impulsively and in dramatic and often drastic ways. Tempers flare, and relationships and agreements will be easily broken. On the other hand, it is a vigorous time, a time of change in which renewed vitality can be injected into failing or lagging ventures. The searing heat of the Tiger year will touch everyone, but it will gradually diminish, and the year will end far more quietly and peacefully than it began.

THE TIGER PERSONALITY

In China, the Tiger represents power, passion, and derring-do, and is revered as the guardian against the three main perils that can afflict a household: fire, thieves, and ghosts.

Tigers are impulsive, energetic, dynamic, and vivacious. Restless and reckless, they are hungry for action and thrive on being the center of attention. Quick-tempered and outspoken about their feelings, they are equally affectionate and generous, and possesses a wonderful sense of humor. They can, however, have suspicious natures, which makes them either prone to wavering indecisiveness—like a cautious, stalking cat—or given to impulsive and rash action. These seeming contradictions are the two main shortcomings in the Tiger's life.

Like their friend the Dog, Tigers are true humanitarians. They are lovers of children, art, music, fine dining, conversation, and anything that stimulates their senses or imaginations.

Their energy, curiosity, and enthusiasm can seem boundless. They have huge egos, and all the fame and success in the world will mean nothing to them if their egos are damaged. They can overlook larger issues while the smallest slight will enrage them. When hindered or defeated, they can become roaring tyrants, the meanest and pettiest of all despots who will go to any lengths, even to burning their own houses down, to get revenge. They will stalk their prey relentlessly, and hell hath no fury as a Tiger scorned. When jealous, they can be overpossessive and quarrelsome.

Rebellious and adventurous, neither materialistic nor security-conscious, all Tigers must have one period in their lives in which they get to act out their impulses and express and find themselves, whether it be by crossing a desert or an ocean or living the Bohemian life in Paris or New York or Tangiers. In their youth, they will passionately pursue the fulfillment of their dreams. Romantic by nature, they need to live life to the fullest. At their positive best they are generous, warm, and sympathetic. At their worst, they are selfish, implacable, obstinate, and unreasonable.

When depressed, Tigers will require copious amounts of sympathy and attention. Don't hold back. They genuinely need it, they will be exceedingly grateful, and you will be amazed at how quickly they recover and proceed undaunted on their chosen course, in spite of whatever advice you may have given them to the contrary.

The female of this sign can be a sleek and elegant feline, a charming and vivacious hostess—but remember, she is a Tigress, and although her claws may be hidden, they are sharp and at the ready should she be crossed or taunted. Although an adventuress, she is also a wonderful and devoted mother. Caring, protective, and nurturing, she will delight in her offspring, as they will in her. They will be entranced by her brilliant smile and her warm and generous nature. She loves to entertain them, dote on them, and educate them. Although it may appear that she spoils them, this is hardly the case. She sees to it that they learn their lessons and follow the rules.

The loyal and reasonable Dog makes an excellent match for the Tiger, appreciative of the Tiger's adventurous and generous spirit and able to advise and restrain the Tiger in practical ways. The Horse makes just as good a partner, sharing the Tiger's lust for life and love of action, while the honest and sanguine Boar will bring security and stability to the Tiger's otherwise volatile existence. Rat, Sheep, Rooster, and another Tiger will also make good matches for the Tiger.

Of all the animal signs, Tigers should avoid the Monkey. This quick-witted and elusive Trickster of Chinese legend cannot help but taunt and enrage the Tiger—and may even take a sadistic delight in doing so. The Tiger will be no match for the Monkey's guile, and will suffer as a result. A union with the Snake is also ill advised. Both signs are equally suspicious, but where the Tiger is rambunctious and forthright, the Snake is silent and deadly. Tigers could also experience bitter clashes with the stubborn and authoritarian Ox, whose horns are capable of wounding them severely.

Tiger children are talkative, inquisitive, and full of energy, capable of being loving and affectionate little cubs and hyperactive and uncontrollable terrors at the same time. Bright, charming, and confident, their eagerness and curiosity are bound to get them into trouble, from which at times they may have to be rescued. But don't worry, they will survive. They just have to find things out for themselves. They express their emotions openly and loudly, so you'll always know what they are feeling. They may dominate their less aggressive peers, but they are also warm, affectionate, generous, and highly gregarious. They must be taught to hold their tempers in check at an early age, and given the right amount of discipline, love, attention, and understanding, the Tiger child, although at times driving you to distraction, can be a source of utter and lasting delight.

THE FIVE TYPES OF TIGERS

Metal Tiger—1950, 2010

Passionate and aggressive, Metal Tigers are utterly sure of what they want and will be tireless and even ruthless about getting it. Self-centered and ostentatious, a spectacle unto themselves, they project a glamorous image. Their actions can be sudden, unorthodox, and radical. They love to act independently and can be overly confident and optimistic in their expectations. They are constant only to themselves and their desires; their hunger and curiosity can lack discernment, and they can be equally susceptible to both good and bad stimuli.

Water Tiger—1902, 1962, 2022

Open-minded realists with calmer natures, who are drawn to new ideas and experiences, these Tigers can be excellent judges of the truth, for they have keen intuitive and communicative abilities. They can be indecisive or procrastinate where action is called for, although they are capable of great concentration once they apply themselves.

Wood Tiger—1914, 1974, 2034

The Wood element gives these Tigers an even disposition. They are affable, practical, and impartial in their judgments. Charming and social animals, they are adroit at bringing people together and at manipulating them to get what they want. Their loyalty, though, is principally to themselves, and no one is indispensable. They can be lacking in self-discipline and have a tendency to shirk responsibility.

Fire Tiger—1926, 1986

Fire Tigers are highly unpredictable and restless creatures, full of volatile and boundless energy, whose actions are bound to be dramatic and forceful and effective. Charismatic, theatrical, and even more expressive than Tigers of other elements, they have strong leadership qualities. They are also extremely generous and optimistic. Passionate and sensual, they live for the present and embrace everything in their lives on a highly personal basis.

Earth Tiger—1938, 1998

These are more practical and less sentimental types of Tiger who rarely allow their emotions to cloud their judgments. Truth is important to them, as are status and recognition; they work diligently to achieve both and are not inclined to take risks or act on impulse. Their relationships (this can include marriage) tend to be more utilitarian in nature, and at times they can appear as mercenary and insensitive.

INFLUENCE OF TIME OF BIRTH

The Hours of the Rat—11 P.M. to 1 A.M.

An excitable Tiger who loves to argue for the sake of argument, a fighter with a loving and sentimental nature, but perhaps less generous when it comes to money.

The Hours of the Ox—1 A.M. to 3 A.M.

This may be a calmer and more disciplined type of Tiger, but with an extremely stubborn, opinionated, and willful disposition.

The Hours of the Tiger—3 A.M. to 5 A.M.

A "pure" Tiger—restless, vivacious, colorful, expressive, independent, and given to intense mood swings.

The Hours of the Rabbit—5 A.M. to 7 A.M.

The Rabbit makes this Tiger less impetuous and impatient and more inclined to caution and good judgment, with a gentler disposition, although he or she is by no means timid or lackluster.

The Hours of the Dragon—7 A.M. to 9 A.M.

A colorful and driven Tiger who could soar to great heights because of the Dragon's high standards and ambition.

The Hours of the Snake—9 A.M. to 11 A.M.

The Snake imparts wisdom and guile to this Tiger, making him or her more inclined to watchful reticence before striking.

The Hours of the Horse—11 A.M. to 1 P.M.

Both signs here are restless, easily stirred, and likely to shun responsibility, although the horse may impart a certain practicality to the Tiger's derring-do.

The Hours of the Sheep—1 P.M. to 3 P.M.

Potentially less aggressive, given to quiet observation, with artistic inclinations, but still capable of being inordinately jealous and possessive.

The Hours of the Monkey—3 P.M. to 5 P.M.

A powerful combination of strength and guile, muscle and intelligence. If the two signs are balanced, this is an individual who will go far.

The Hours of the Rooster—5 P.M. to 7 P.M.

Tigers with a colorful flair—not that they don't have that already—who make a point of being heard—not that they don't do that already, either. They have a sharp and discerning eye, at least where others are concerned, and no one is left off the hook.

The Hours of the Dog—7 P.M. to 9 P.M.

A more reasonable Tiger who is imbued with the Dog's open-mindedness and sense of fair play, although this big cat's tongue may at times be as sharp as its claws, especially when attacked or wounded.

The Hours of the Boar—9 P.M. to 11 P.M.

The Tiger's impetuousness is combined with the Boar's naiveté. An easygoing and contented creature who nonetheless could become vindictive when thwarted or the going gets rough.

The Year of the Boar—2007

The prosperity that marks the beginning of this year does not last. Tigers must be wary of new associates and high-risk ventures.

The Year of the Rat—2008

A difficult year for business. Money is hard to come by, and Tigers must avoid acting on impulse.

The Year of the Ox—2009

A frustrating year, in which Tigers may find their plans and aspirations hindered or blocked by someone in authority, leading to quarrels and misunderstandings. A time for Tigers to curb their impatience and temper. Their troubles will pass if they can maintain a cool head in the face of adversity.

The Year of the Tiger—2010

This is not a good year to take any risks. Tigers may find that they have to spend money rather than make it, but are fortunate in that others come to their aid when they need it.

The Year of the Rabbit—2011

A good year for both business and romance, and Tigers will find contentment in their overall achievements.

Unhappiness could come as the result of separation from a loved one or the breakup of a partnership. It will be hard to raise money, and Tigers could be persuaded to make unwise investments.

The Year of the Snake—2013

Progress is steady this year, although with no significant gains. Neither are there any significant losses. The Tigers' main troubles will come from members of the opposite sex.

The Year of the Horse—2014

A very good year in which money comes easily and great gains are in store.

The Year of the Sheep—2015

There are no serious problems this year; Tigers could find themselves preoccupied with difficult negotiations, tensions at work, and family disputes. They could also suffer the loss of some personal belongings.

The Year of the Monkey—2016

A difficult year, in which Tigers experience many setbacks and irritations. A time to avoid confrontations and legal disputes.

The Year of the Rooster—2017

Problems loom, but Tigers should not give in to anxiety, as help comes from unexpected sources and newfound friends.

The Year of the Dog—2018

A protected time, although Tigers will have to work hard if they are to be successful and will feel frustrated by the limitations that are placed upon them. However, luck comes through the support of influential people who aid them in their plans.

SOME FAMOUS TIGERS

Pierre Balmain, Ludwig van Beethoven, Simon Bolívar, Emily Brontë, Roger Corman, Charles de Gaulle, Giscard D'Estaing, Vittorio De Sica, Isadora Duncan, Marguerite Duras, Dwight D. Eisenhower, Queen Elizabeth II, Sir Alec Guinness, Hugh Hefner, Ho Chi Minh, John Houseman, Norman Jewison, Jessica Lange, Gypsy Rose Lee, Karl Malden, Groucho Marx, Victor Mature, Marilyn Monroe, Philip Noyce, Rudolph Nureyev, Oliver Reed, Diana Rigg, John Schlesinger, Romy Schneider, Jean Seberg, Cybill Shepherd, Tennessee Williams, Stevie Wonder.

four

THE RABBIT

Chinese Name: Tù
Direction: East
Fixed Element: Wood
Stem: Negative
Western Sign: Pisces
Color: Grey
Flower: Rose
Fragrance: Shalimar
Tree: Poplar
Birthstone: Sapphire
Lucky Number: 4

Years of the Rabbit: 1951, 1963, 1975, 1987, 1999, 2011, 2023

THE YEAR OF THE RABBIT

A tranquil year; a time to rest and recuperate after the turmoil and upheavals of the year of the Tiger. People will be inclined to avoid any unpleasantness, and good manners, diplomacy, and gentle persuasion will be the rule of the day. Life will move at a leisurely pace while at the same time money can be made without strenuous effort.

THE RABBIT PERSONALITY

The agile Hares leap over or slip around any obstacles in their paths. They have remarkable resilience, enabling them always to recover from whatever calamities might befall them. In Chinese mythology, the Rabbit or Hare is the symbol of longevity. In Chinese paintings, they are often depicted with a large vat, in which they are preparing the elixir of life. The Rabbit is said to derive its essence from the moon, and the story of the Hare in the Moon is one of the famous "lost legends" of China. The Moon Rabbit is a major figure in the Chinese Mid-autumn Festival. The Western Easter Rabbit is the product of a similar belief in the Moon Rabbit from pre-Christian times; the egg is a symbol of fertility. The Rabbit or Hare has ancient and universal associations with the Easter season, or spring equinox, and the Chinese calendar is always arranged so that the spring equinox occurs within the Rabbit month.

The Rabbit is regarded as one of the most fortunate signs in the Chinese horoscope, deemed the most likely to find happiness and contentment in life. Those born under this sign are the epitome of graciousness, good manners, kindness, sound judg-ment, refinement, and aestheticism. They are likely to live tran-quil lives (depending on the hour of their birth) in a quiet and peaceful environment. They have artistic natures and are lovers of beauty. The are also extremely lucky in business and mone-tary transactions, adroit at making deals to their own advan-tage. Sophisticated and self-indulgent and lovers of leisure, their creature comforts are very important to them, and they always put their own desires first. They value themselves above all else, and will discard anything or anyone they find too demanding or upsetting to the much-valued tranquillity of their existence. They loathe discomfort of any sort. In fact, security and com-fort could become an obsession with some Rabbits. Although kind and considerate to their loved ones, they can be ruthless in their dealings with outsiders and can demonstrate a fiendish cunning. They are inscrutable negotiators whose thoughts can be impossible to read. Although they appear docile on the sur-face, their gentle and unobtrusive manner conceals a strong will that quietly and methodically pursues its goals with caution and discretion.

At their worst, Rabbits can be overly sensitive and imagina-tive. They will always be disarmingly civil and polite, even to their worst enemies, while concealing a dark and brooding ani-mosity. Private and highly secretive, they can resort to subversive means to bring down anyone they feel is a threat. Joseph Stalin and Fidel Castro are both Rabbits. Rabbits also have a tendency to hedge around issues and shift the blame onto others.

Rabbits have an acute distaste for conflict or confrontation of any sort. They are at heart avowed pacifists. They don't understand why people can't simply be polite and get along. They are also equipped with an acute and agile sense of knowing how to stay out of harm's way. They are ultimate survivalists. As friends, they will certainly lend you money when you need it, but do not count on them for anything more. They're certainly willing to take you to the river; just don't ask them to swim across it with you. They are prone to be moody, and can appear withdrawn or even completely detached from those around them.

At their best, Rabbits are sophisticated, urbane, and intelligent, sympathetic listeners and marvelous hosts. They also have a knack for accurately remembering details that others might overlook or forget. They are extremely thorough, and often make good scholars. They will be admired and sought after for their impeccable manners, graciousness, wit, sound advice, and refined taste. Their innate detachment and self-assurance makes them tolerant and nonjudgmental; they believe in "Live and let live," and living is something they know how to do well. They have great finesse, and are excellent hosts and entertainers.

The female Rabbit is composed and very feminine. She is gentle, considerate, and understanding, and her friends find her warm and delightful and very energetic and enthusiastic about the things she likes to do. She loves, indeed needs, to be pampered, and the man she marries will be required to provide her with the luxuries and security she believes she needs as well as cater to her more sullen moods.

Rabbit children are sweet, obedient, and even-tempered. They are easy to discipline and are able to quietly concentrate on one thing at time. They are very sensitive to the moods of their parents and the emotional climate of the household, and know instinctively how to act to protect themselves and not make any waves. They are able to mask their feelings, and at times may be difficult to read. They will not be openly defiant, but this does not mean they are not willful. They know what to say and do to get their way or bargain for a better deal. They learn their way around people and problems at an early age, and can deal philosophically with any setbacks that come their way.

The Rabbit will make the best of all possible matches with a person born in the year of the Sheep. They share much in common, and will make a lasting and very successful union. The sensual, easygoing Boar and the honest, fair-minded Dog will make equally good partners for the Rabbit. The Rat, Ox, Dragon, Snake, Monkey, or another Rabbit will make good secondary matches. The Rabbit should avoid any relationship with the Rooster, whose vanity and harsh criticism the Rabbit will find intolerable. Rabbits will be equally unimpressed by the rash and imposing Tiger, and exacerbated by the temperamental and capricious Horse.

Metal Rabbit—1951, 2011

These Rabbits are physically and mentally stronger than Rabbits of other elements. They have unwavering belief in their own judgments and abilities, are less likely to compromise, and are more inclined to assume responsibility and show initiative in work. Metal makes them highly preoccupied with their goals and desires. They are especially cunning and ambitious, which is well-masked by their cool logic and intelligence. Although often indifferent to the opinions of others, they are openly moved by beauty and any well-executed form of creative expression. They are ardent lovers and devoted workers and can be inclined to dark moods.

Water Rabbit—1903, 1963, 2023

Empathics with emotional and fragile natures, Water Rabbits are highly sensitive to their environments and the thoughts and feelings of others. As a result, they cannot bear any form of conflict. On the other hand, they are able to unconsciously transmit their ideas to others and draw them to them, and are often surprised by the support they receive. In their negative moods, they can dwell too much on past injuries, indulge in self-pity, be plagued by dark imaginings that make them highly suspicious of others' motives, and become incommunicative.

Wood Rabbit—1915, 1975, 2035

This is a double Wood sign (Wood is the Rabbit's fixed element), that could produce generous and sympathetic Rabbits who at times may be too charitable and permissive for their own good, allowing others to take advantage of them. They thrive in corporate or institutional settings, where they will steadily and diplomatically climb the ladder of success. Because of their desire to fit in and not offend, they may hedge or hide behind bureaucratic red tape, often hurting themselves as well as others as a result. They must learn to be more decisive and discriminating in order to protect themselves.

Fire Rabbit—1927, 1987, 2047

Fire makes these Rabbits temperamental, demonstrative, and affectionate, although they are still able to mask their emotions with the Rabbit's outward guise of detachment. They are reputed to have more strength of character than Rabbits of other elements, and they are gifted with leadership qualities, but these too are tempered by diplomacy and moderation. In negotiations they will use indirect methods, such as go-betweens and secret liaisons, in order to get the deal done. At times they may be outspoken and emotional, but, like all Rabbits, confrontation is the last thing they desire. When negative, they can be easily angered or hurt and prone to neurosis.

Earth Rabbit—1939, 1999

Earth makes these Rabbits serious, steadfast, and constant, and less inclined to be ruled by their emotions. They deliberate before they move, and their actions are always well calculated. They are introverted creatures who turn inward to deal with their problems. They are materialistic and primarily concerned with their own well-being, although they will recognize and strive to overcome their flaws.

INFLUENCE OF TIME OF BIRTH

The Hours of the Rat—11 P.M. to 1 A.M.

A lively and affectionate Rabbit, shrewd, informed, and less indifferent to others.

The Hours of the Ox—1 A.M. to 3 A.M.

The Ox imbues this Rabbit with more authority, steadfastness, and strength than one might otherwise expect from the normally timorous Hare.

Hours of the Tiger—3 A.M. to 5 A.M.

A more aggressive and quick-witted Rabbit, imbued with the Tiger's impulsive energy while at the same time able to keep it under control.

The Hours of the Rabbit—5 A.M. to 7 A.M.

A "double" or "pure" Rabbit. A philosophical pacifist who rarely, if ever, takes sides. True believers in Buddhist "non-action," they know how to take good care of themselves.

The Hours of the Dragon—7 A.M. to 9 A.M.

Ambitious and hard-nosed Rabbits who are able to inspire and command others to carry out their plans.

The Hours of the Snake—9 A.M. to 11 A.M.

Self-sufficient, reflective, and mutable Rabbits who are highly intuitive and sensitive to their surroundings.

The Hours of the Horse—11 A.M. to 1 P.M.

A more outgoing, self-confident, and spirited Rabbit, with a happy disposition.

The Hours of the Sheep—1 P.M. to 3 P.M.

Generous, sympathetic, and tolerant Rabbits who are capable of loving others as much as themselves.

The Hours of the Monkey—3 P.M. to 5 P.M.

A mischievous and conniving Rabbit, full of laughter and tricks. The Rabbit's cool diplomacy and finesse is matched with the Monkey's charm and guile—a master dealmaker and escape artist.

The Hours of the Rooster—5 P.M. to 7 P.M.

Given the Rabbit's sensitive insight and the Rooster's judgment, this combination has an eloquence that demands attention.

The Hours of the Dog—7 P.M. to 9 P.M.

More involved and moralistic types of Rabbit, whose acute sensitivity coupled with the Dog's sense of justice could make them more aggressive and outspoken on social issues and the welfare of others.

The Hours of the Boar—9 P.M. to 11 P.M.

The Boar's easygoing ways and gregariousness could make these Rabbits less selfish and more concerned with the welfare of those around them, especially in terms of their own self-interest, and as long as those others are ready to adapt to and not disrupt the comfort of their surroundings.

THE RABBIT'S PROSPECTS IN COMING YEARS

The Year of the Boar—2007

Rabbits should avoid making promises or commitments this year, as unforeseen difficulties are likely to come at them as though out of thin air. They must be very realistic and cautious and take the necessary steps to protect themselves.

The Year of the Rat—2008

A calm year for the Rabbit, with no problems or surprises. Progress is steady, although not particularly fruitful.

The Year of the Ox—2009

Rabbits could face some health problems this year as the result of anxiety and the loss of or separation from a loved one. They are beset by disappointments and hard work that bears little fruit. A year to lie low and not try to implement any moves or changes.

The Year of the Tiger—2010

A distasteful and disturbing year, in which Rabbits must exercise more than their usual caution to avoid conflicts and disputes. They must also be wary where money and investments are involved. Gains will be made toward the end of the year.

The Year of the Rabbit—2011

A most auspicious year. Financial gains, promotions, recognition, and unexpected benefits are foreseen, along with happy developments and celebrations at home.

The Year of the Dragon—2012

A mixed year money-wise, Rabbits will be reasonably happy and busy at home. They could make powerful new friends, and their gains will outweigh their losses.

The Year of the Snake—2013

Difficulties come at Rabbits from several directions this year, and it will be hard for them to make any tangible progress. A change of residence or a new job are distinct possibilities, and they may be faced with some unplanned expenses.

The Year of the Horse—2014

A good year, in which luck comes from meeting influential and helpful people. Losses are recouped, and there could be much traveling and entertaining.

The Year of the Sheep—2015

A prosperous year, in which plans go smoothly and much is accomplished.

The Year of the Monkey—2016

Financial deals and contracts could be tricky this year or meet with unexpected delays; the Rabbit should be wary of being betrayed by a close ally.

The Year of the Rooster—2017

A difficult year beset by problems at home and at work. Rabbits should not try to act independently, but seek the help of others to support them. Their tribulations will be overcome, but not without anxiety and frustration.

Gains will be made and problems sorted out, although Rabbits may well be the target of criticism by superiors or hindered in some way by those around them.

SOME FAMOUS RABBITS

Harry Belafonte, Ingrid Bergman, Claudia Cardinale, Fidel Castro, Francis Ford Coppola, Albert Einstein, Peter Falk, David Frost, Cary Grant, Jomo Kenyatta, Nancy Kwan, Gina Lollobrigida, Ali McGraw, Henry Miller, France Nuyen, David Rockefeller, Ken Russell, George C. Scott, Benjamin Spock, Joseph Stalin, Meryl Streep, Queen Victoria, Johannes Vorster, Orson Welles, Zhang Yimou.

five

THE DRAGON

Chinese Name: Long
Direction: East-Southeast
Fixed Element: Wood
Stem: Positive
Western Sign: Aries
Color: Gold
Flower: Rose
Fragrance: Eau Verte
Tree: Sequoia
Birthstone: Ruby
Lucky Number: 2
Years of the Dragon: 1952, 1964, 1976, 1988, 2000, 2012

THE YEAR OF THE DRAGON

An expansive, combustible, energetic, and exhilarating year, in which caution is thrown to the wind and grandiose schemes and ventures are embarked upon. Everything and everyone is touched this year by the Dragon's indomitable spirit and colossal ambition and daring. Money will be easily obtained, as big spending and speculation will be the rule of the day. This is indeed a time to act, as great things can and will be done, but we must also be cautious lest, like Icarus, we fly too close to the sun and come crashing down on melting wings. Fortunes as well as disasters will come in huge waves, and tempers will erupt as people and even nations rebel against constrictions and injustice of every sort. As there is nothing mediocre about the Dragon, successes as well as failures will be manifested on a grand scale.

The Chinese regard this as a most auspicious year to launch a new business, get married, or have children, as the mighty and benevolent Dragon is the harbinger of happiness and good fortune.

THE DRAGON PERSONALITY

In China, the Dragon is the symbol of the emperor or Yang—male—energy. The Dragon is the guardian of wealth and power. Like its close relative the Snake (often referred to as "the little Dragon"), the Dragon is a karmic sign, and those born in the Dragon year are said to wear the "horns of destiny."

Proud, aristocratic, eccentric, egotistical, and extremely forthright and direct, Dragons will establish their goals and ideals quite early in life. They set high standards for themselves and have the potential to accomplish great things. They possess little to no self-doubt, and are courageous, individualistic, and pioneering. Inspired by their own grandiose and colorful visions, whatever they attempt will be either stupendous, trail-blazing successes or dramatic failures. For them there is no safe or middle road, only victory or death. Whatever their chosen path, they must follow it, regardless of the consequences. They were born with a mission in life, and it is their destiny to fulfill it. Zealous and impetuous, full of vitality and strength, Dragons are veritable storehouses of dynamic energy. However, they must learn to temper their early enthusiasm, as they could run the risk of seeing everything burn up like a meteor.

While he or she may be magnanimous, strong, and decisive, the straightforward and truthful Dragon is distinctly lacking in cunning or guile. In a sense, Dragons regard such ways as beneath them, and in their pride and aloofness they may neglect to pay attention to the subversive or deceitful ways of those around them. They operate on strength and truth alone, and cannot understand why others don't do the same and meet them fair and square. Often this is because they can intimidate, even when they don't mean to, for in a direct confrontation the Dragon is incontestable, an indomitable champion of the joust, a chivalrous but unbeatable opponent.

Strong-tempered and often a raging sea of emotions when crossed (the sea is the Dragon's ancestral home), Dragons are just as quick to forgive and forget once they have let off steam (or smoke). They can be breathing fire on you one minute and then tenderly dressing your wounds the next, believing that you have learned your lesson or, at the very least, that they have been heard. Although imperious and dogmatic, they are at heart true believers in personal dignity, individual freedom, and human rights—kings or queens who know that to rule is to serve—although it may at times appear that they believe themselves to be above the law. Filial and generous by nature, whatever differences or conflicts they may have with their families or friends will be immediately set aside when they call for help. Dragons seldom waver or lie, and it will be hard for you not to place your confidence in them. They are open people. You can read them like a book. It is difficult for them to hide their feelings, and they rarely try to do so. Why should they bother? Their emotions are genuine and straight from the heart, and when they say they love you, you can be sure they mean it.

Being diplomatic and soft-spoken can be difficult for the Dragon. Should they belong to the less refined type, their direct approach can appear as brusque and even abrasive, offending and antagonizing people who see them as egocentric and arrogant. In spite of this shortcoming, their presence and magnetism inspire and motivate those around them, and they will have a great number of admirers who support and believe in them. Their greatest pitfalls are overconfidence in their own abilities and refusal to accept to defeat. They will spend all of their resources before admitting to failure. They need to learn when to retreat and when to guard their flanks.

The female Dragon is the Empress Dowager herself, the archetypal matriarch as well as woman-warrior, a builder and burner of cities (Joan of Arc was a Dragon). She is totally emancipated and independent-minded, and considers herself equal to any man, if not better. She is a regal, straightforward, and practical individual who is strictly to the point. This aspect of her personality will be expressed in her dress, which will be elegant in its simplicity. She seldom bothers with unnecessary adornment—the brilliance of her being is more than enough to tell you who she is.

Dragon children are high-spirited, energetic, fearless, forceful, and emotionally intense. They are likely to wander off dauntlessly into snake-infested woods or start swimming across the river, unable to comprehend the panic they are causing among the adults watching over them. They establish their principles and ideals at an early age, and act accordingly to prove their worth, both to themselves and to their parents and teachers. They will have innumerable idols and role models as they grow. Their dreams of greatness are real and tangible to them, and their efforts to perform and improve themselves are sincere and should be encouraged and praised. Their self-esteem is extremely important to them. Their emotions are intense, and ridicule can hurt them deeply. These children are, after all, their own worst critics. They judge themselves harshly, and if they make a mistake they'll be the first to see it. Dragon children were born to lead and excel at whatever they do, and they are self-reliant, proud, and absolutely true to their ideals.

The Dragon will be attracted first and foremost to the charming and irresistible Monkey, whose guile and wit are a perfect complement to the Dragon's brave-hearted honesty and power. The Monkey likewise will be drawn to the Dragon's majesty, strength, and dynamic energy. The Monkey is the wise court jester and advisor to the Dragon-king (or queen). They will find a deep affinity and mutual love and understanding, and make a happy and successful team. A Dragon-Rat union will be equally as winning, and the Dragon will also make a good match with the wise, alluring, and serenely elegant but practical Snake, who will be able to quietly temper the Dragon's excesses.

Ox, Tiger, Rabbit, Sheep, Horse, Boar, and another Dragon each make good secondary matches. Only the Dog will make a miserable match for the Dragon. The Dog will be highly critical and mistrustful of the Dragon and cast a cynical pall over his or her grandiose designs.

THE FIVE TYPES OF DRAGONS

Metal Dragon—1940, 2000

This is perhaps the most determined and strong-willed of all the Dragons, who values honesty and integrity above all else—a great virtue but one which can also make them inflexible and overly critical. They may be fanatical about their beliefs, and they are able to intimidate less aggressive or weaker individuals into submitting to their will. They are decidedly action-oriented and combative, and will stake their lives on their convictions. When negative, they can be excessively self-important and stubborn, and will go it alone when others refuse to accept their leadership.

Water Dragon—1952, 2012

Water has a calming and beneficial effect, making these Dragons less imperious, egotistical, and power-hungry than Dragons of other elements. Theirs is a "live and let live" philosophy. They believe firmly in individual freedom and dignity and "To thine own self be true." They have formidable willpower and are capable of marketing their ideas with ceaseless dedication. Keen and intuitive observers, they know when and where to apply force and are subsequently very successful negotiators. Tolerant and liberal-minded, they can accept rejection or defeat without rancor. They are progressive, expansive, growth-oriented, and patient in their outlook and know how to act wisely to achieve their goals. Their fundamental flaw is that they can be overly optimistic, trying to accomplish too much at once while risking everything in the process.

Wood Dragon—1904, 1964, 2024

These Dragons' every action will be guided by well thought-out logic. They are good at formulating and applying their ideas and at developing innovative and revolutionary concepts. Less fierce and domineering than other Dragons, they work well with others and are able to compromise when it is to their advantage, but can be prone to endless and tiresome debate when opposed. Like all Dragons, they are proud, outspoken, and fearless when challenged.

Fire Dragon—1916, 1976, 2036

The most competitive, aggressive, and upright of all the Dragons, they have tremendous energy coupled with a zealousness that can verge on the fanatical. They have great leadership qualities, but these can be blemished by their tendencies to be martinets with Messiah complexes. In spite of this, they are open and humane and impartial seekers of the truth, able to inspire others to soar with them to great heights. When negative, they can be short-tempered, ruthlessly ambitious, intolerant, and inconsiderate.

Earth Dragon—1928, 1988

These gregarious, executive, and autocratic Dragons are nonetheless fair-minded and open and appreciative of other points of view even when they don't necessarily agree with them. Earth makes them realistic and objective. They have a proclivity to subjugate others and a desire to be in control of their environments, but they are also reasonable and less dictatorial than Dragons of other elements. They are tireless workers who will labor incessantly to improve their talents and maximize their potential. These aristocratic individuals are quiet, strong, and courageous and less inclined to temperamental outbursts.

INFLUENCE OF TIME OF BIRTH

The Hours of the Rat—11 P.M. to 1 A.M.

The Dragon's innate generosity may be tempered by the Rat's frugality, and the Rat's caution and sentimental and affectionate nature may make this individual inclined to be subjective and indecisive.

The Hours of the Ox—1 A.M. to 3 A.M.

A stolid, slow-moving Dragon, who can be extremely stubborn and forceful when challenged or crossed.

The Hours of the Tiger—3 A.M. to 5 A.M.

The Tiger makes this Dragon impulsive, restless, impatient, and generous to a fault. This person may be suspicious and indecisive as well, and could be reckless and even hysterical, but he or she will be a compulsive worker.

The Hours of the Rabbit—5 A.M. to 7 A.M.

These quiet and debonair Dragons are given to reflection before they act. Here strength and diplomacy are well blended. May be more luxury-loving than most other Dragons.

The Hours of the Dragon—7 A.M. to 9 A.M.

He or She Who-Must-Be-Obeyed. An imperious and commanding individual who demands attention and devotion. His or her word is an imperial or even religious edict, not to be questioned.

The Hours of the Snake—9 A.M. to 11 A.M.

Precise and secretive Dragons who plot every move they make. The Snake's charm and quiet allure masks their intensity and ruthless ambition.

The Hours of the Horse—11 A.M. to 1 P.M.

The Horse's capricious selfishness may override the Dragon's generosity and sense of duty. A gregarious and fast-talking high-stakes gambler.

The Hours of the Sheep—1 P.M. to 3 P.M.

An understanding and modest Dragon who knows how to get things done without applying brute force. A good negotiator with artistic inclinations.

The Hours of the Monkey—3 P.M. to 5 P.M.

Witty and dazzling court jesters—but don't let them fool you. They are a formidable combination of strength and guile, the Tricksters who see through all lies.

A colorful, imaginative, and fearless Dragon whose pride is immeasurable and who may have a certain preening vanity.

The Hours of the Dog—7 P.M. to 9 P.M.

A practical, down-to-earth but good-humored Dragon, but who may have a nasty bite or acid tongue when attacked.

The Hours of the Boar—9 P.M. to 11 P.M.

A warmhearted, sensual, and generous Dragon, who will be a devoted and faithful friend.

THE DRAGON'S PROSPECTS IN COMING YEARS

The Year of the Boar—2007

Luck shines once again on the Dragon. Business or finances show mixed results, but the Dragon encounters few major problems, and family life is trouble-free.

The Year of the Rat—2008

A very good year for both business and romance. No major problems at home or at work, although Dragons must still be careful, as one bad deal would deplete their resources.

The Year of the Ox—2009

Although progress is moderate, this is still a fortunate year for Dragons, as they are protected from the numerous conflicts and troubles that seem to surround them.

The Year of the Tiger—2010

The Dragons' plans are blocked or hampered by others, and they find it difficult to get anything substantial accomplished. Their home lives are also disturbed by sad news or the loss or departure of a loved one.

The Year of the Rabbit—2011

A good and calm year. A stable time in which fair progress in business is foreseen. The Dragons' domestic life is peaceful and stable, although they could experience some minor health problems.

The Year of the Dragon—2012

An excellent year, in which success comes easily. Dragons could acquire both fame and fortune.

The Year of the Snake—2013

The luck of the Dragon year continues, although they may encounter some minor opposition and experience romantic problems as home life is neglected.

The Year of the Horse—2014

A year marked by uncertainty and unpleasant surprises, although problems will be resolved if Dragons do not overreact.

The Year of the Sheep—2015

Progress is moderate with no significant gains in career or finances. Home life is peaceful and free of disruption or any negative disturbances.

The Year of the Monkey—2016

Progress is foreseen in career and finances, but Dragons must still be careful to avoid legal entanglements. There is the danger of broken friendships or romantic strife if the Dragon is too headstrong.

The Year of the Rooster—2017

A year marked by good news, recognition, financial gain, and social advancement.

The Year of the Dog—2018

A difficult year, filled with unexpected problems and hindrances in which Dragons must be careful to avoid confronting their enemies.

Bernardo Bertolucci, Shirley Temple Black, Rosemary Clooney, Jimmy Connors, Joan Crawford, Chen Kaige, Bing Crosby, Salvador Dali, Willem de Kooning, Kirk Douglas, Glenn Ford, Francisco Franco, Jean Gabin, Jackie Gleason, Graham Greene, Ché Guevara, Mark Hamill, Lawrence Harvey, Sterling Hayden, Edward Heath, Trevor Howard, Joan of Arc, Eartha Kitt, Stanley Kubrick, John Lennon, Peter Lorre, Gabriel García Marquez, Walter Mondale, Roger Moore, Jeanne Moreau, Yehudi Menuhin, Gregory Peck, Tony Richardson, Anthony Quinn, Haile Selassie, Frank Sinatra, Ringo Starr, Mae West, Harold Wilson.

six

THE SNAKE

Chinese Name: Shé
Direction: South-Southeast
Fixed Element: Fire
Stem: Negative
Western Sign: Taurus
Color: Light blue
Flower: Camellia
Fragrance: Musk
Tree: Palm
Birthstone: Opal
Lucky Number: 3
Years of the Snake: 1953, 1965, 1977, 1989, 2001, 2013

THE YEAR OF THE SNAKE

This year appears tranquil on the surface, but in actuality many of the disasters and calamities whose seeds were sown during the excesses of the Year of the Dragon manifest themselves in the Year of the Snake. The Snake likes to resolve conflicts, and if no peaceful settlement can be reached, then the Snake will attack. (Japan's sneak attack on Pearl Harbor was in the Year of the Snake, and Admiral Yamamoto expressed his fear that they had "awakened a sleeping dragon.") It is, however, a most auspicious year for commerce, industry, science, technology, and the arts. Solutions and comprises are reached, with a great deal of thoughtful negotiation and mistrust. It is also a vigorous time for courtship, romance, and scandals of every sort. Music and theater flourish, and sophisticated elegance is the rule of the day. This is a year marked by unpredictability. The Snake appears to move slowly, but once roused he strikes like lightning.

THE SNAKE PERSONALITY

This is the most enigmatic and mystical sign of the Chinese zodiac, endowed with innate wisdom and a mysterious allure. It is said that the most beautiful women and powerful men are born under this sign. Both the Snake's thinking and emotions run very deep. In their relationships with others they can be possessive and demanding, and they will never forgive a promise broken or a wrong done. Once roused to anger their hatred can be vicious and unrelenting—and it is silent, cold, and deadly. The Sicilian adage, "Revenge is a dish best served cold," must have been coined by a Snake.

Above all, the charismatic Snake has a profound sense of responsibility and enduring purpose. Like their cousin the Dragon, they are born to lead and soar to great heights.

Snakes are by nature skeptical and mistrusting, and inclined to be somewhat superstitious. Like the Dragon, theirs is a karmic sign, and it is their destiny to pay all dues and settle all scores before they leave this life. They can be deeply religious and even psychic or, on the other extreme, totally hedonistic and materialistic. Money comes easily to them, and they are rarely bothered by financial woes. Snakes can also be quite generous, but they can be ruthless in eliminating anyone who stands between them and their goals.

There is no anticipating a Snake's next move—they are constantly calculating and plotting. They are highly secretive and very careful about what they say. Shrewd and prudent, they are adept in business and financial transactions and can also make excellent politicians. They understand and desire power, and beneath their outward cloak of serenity are always alert and on guard. Their philosophical bent allows them a refined sense of humor as well as considerable grace under pressure. In times of adversity, they can be relied upon to remain calm and maintain their presence of mind. They deal with misfortune with a calm assurance and intrepidity. They are remarkably resilient. In the event of a catastrophe, they are able to shed their skins and reemerge with a new and even more resplendent one, almost as if by magic.

Snakes of both sexes are characteristically blessed with beautiful complexions. Under their cool demeanors, they are high-strung, finely tuned individuals. As they keep their emotions inward and hidden, the tension they feel affects their digestive and nervous systems, and they can be prone to stomach ulcers and other digestive ailments.

The female Snake is more often than not a sleek, serene, and enticing beauty, sensuous, graceful, and languid in her movements and manner. She is confident, collected, and poised, and her effect can be quietly mesmerizing. She will love jewelry—as long as it is the real thing—and her tastes are sophisticated and singularly elegant. She is fully aware of her mysterious allure and aura of sexual intrigue. Equality of the sexes is not an issue with her. Hers is an ancient female power—the snake-goddess personified—and she has no need to compete with men when it is so easy to entice them into doing her bidding.

Like all Snakes, she admires the power and influence that come with money and will have high standards for a mate. If her husband has not yet attained her goals, she will dedicate herself to seeing that he does, working behind the scenes, dressing the part, playing the perfect hostess, offering shrewd advice, and exercising her hypnotic charm.

All Snakes are passionate lovers, with reputedly strong sexual appetites. In fact, they pursue all objects of their desire with the same covetous fervor. They often—especially those with an insatiable lust for power or fame—lead dangerous lives full of intrigue and excitement.

Snake children are reticent, pensive, intelligent, and alert. They know what they want and are very practical in establishing their goals. They are careful and attentive and know how to avoid trouble. Secretive and brooding, they hide their pain and are capable of bearing grudges for a long time. They are often misunderstood because, being Snakes, they are enigmas who refuse or fail to communicate successfully with those around them. However, they are charismatic, and other children will look to them for leadership. Gifted with a high IQ and a natural aptitude for learning, a Snake is able to discipline himself and has remarkable focus.

The Snake will make the best partnership with the stalwart and reliable Ox, the audacious and colorful Rooster, and the illustrious and straightforward Dragon. Rat, Rabbit, Sheep, and Dog or another Snake will all make good secondary matches.

The Snake and the Boar are diametrically opposed to each other, and such a union is ill advised. Where the Snake is secretive, polished, sophisticated, and complex, the Boar is mundane, straightforward, and simplistic. These two will never understand each other, and their conflicts will be deep and long-lasting—they are natural enemies. The defiant and willful Tiger will clash with the Snake's secretive and discerning ways, and they will be mutually suspicious of each other. The wily Monkey will oppose the Snake with its own form of cunning, and the two are likely to engage in an ongoing cloak-and-dagger war, each trying to catch the other unaware. The Snake will experience cold and distant relations at best with the fickle, impulsive, and equally demanding Horse, whose capricious ways will offend the Snake's refined and subtle sensibilities. Snakes will find Horses loud, selfish, arrogant (which they do not find the Dragon, for all of its grandiose sounding off) and even stupid in their ways.

THE FIVE TYPES OF SNAKE

Metal Snake—1941, 2001

The most secretive and elusive of all the Snakes, mistrustful of others and gifted with a calculating intelligence and strong willpower. Metal makes them crave opulence and luxury, and they will be steadfast in their devotion to the acquisition of wealth and power. They move with great stealth, and are not above using underhanded means to subdue their opponents. They can be possessive and domineering, but also generous and cooperative.

Water Snake—1953, 2013

A charismatic Snake with great mental abilities, insightfulness, powers of concentration, and business acumen. Shrewd, practical, and materialistic, but also well read and artistic, they are adroit at managing both people and finances. Calm and unperturbed on the surface, these Snakes' emotions run very deep; they have long memories and can harbor lifetime grievances.

Wood Snake—1905, 1965, 2025

Wood combined with the Snake's fixed element of Fire will make these individuals shine like a flame, attracting rather than pursuing the people and objects they desire. Their tastes and habits will be expensive, and they will crave admiration and approval. Both emotional and financial security are important to them, and they will work hard to achieve lasting success. Their affections, also, are constant and enduring, although they will demand complete intellectual freedom. They have an almost prophetic understanding of the course of events and of their own time and place in history.

Fire Snake—1917, 1977

Fire gives these individuals great charisma and energy, with an aura of confident leadership. They have a strong desire for fame, wealth, and power, and can be uncompromising and relentless in the pursuit of their goals, which tend to be very high. They are ardent and sensual and can be excessively jealous. They love and hate with the same intensity, and are suspicious by nature and often quick to judge and condemn.

Earth Snake—1929, 1989

Warm and spontaneous, Earth Snakes are principled and reliable and form slow and correct judgments. They rely on their own opinions and integrity and refuse to be intimidated by the crowd. Disarmingly graceful and charming, they will have many admirers and will be intensely loyal to their friends. They are hard-working, organized, and frugal with money, and know how to set their own limits and operate successfully within them.

INFLUENCE OF TIME OF BIRTH

The Hours of the Rat—11 P.M. to 1 A.M.

An affable and charming Snake, with the Rat's sentimentality and love of money, could be a real go-getter and hustler.

The Hours of the Ox—1 A.M. to 3 A.M.

A very formidable Snake—the Ox's stamina and stubborn willpower are concealed by the Snake's hypnotic charm and elusiveness.

The Hours of the Tiger—3 A.M. to 5 A.M.

A warm and versatile individual who is also hyper-suspicious.

The Hours of the Rabbit—5 A.M. to 7 A.M.

A genial, debonair, well-mannered Snake, adept at making deals but a with poisonous bite concealed beneath a genteel exterior.

The Hours of the Dragon—7 A.M. to 9 A.M.

Here wisdom and power come together—the Snake will commit totally to whatever cause he or she adopts.

The Hours of the Snake—9 A.M. to 11 A.M.

An elusive yet enchanting creature of great enigma and intrigue—possessive and relentless—once this Snake bites onto something it will never let go.

The Hours of the Horse—11 A.M. to 1 P.M.

This combination makes for a humorous, charming, and highly amorous individual.

The Hours of the Sheep—1 P.M. to 3 P.M.

An artistic Snake with expensive tastes; capable of great cunning beneath a gentle and friendly demeanor.

The Hours of the Monkey—3 P.M. to 5 P.M.

Guile, wisdom, glamour, charm, and wit are combined in an individual who is virtually impossible to resist.

The Hours of the Rooster—5 P.M. to 7 P.M.

A plumed serpent, knowledgeable and persistent, with an obsessive desire for power beneath those colorful feathers.

The Hours of the Dog—7 P.M. to 9 P.M.

Possibly a slightly less secretive and forthright Snake, with the Dog's strong moral sense.

The Hours of the Boar—9 P.M. to 11 P.M.

A hedonistic and sensual bon vivant who could be something of a good-willed Dionysus, but still shrewd when dealing with others.

THE SNAKE'S PROSPECTS IN COMING YEARS

The Year of the Boar—2007

The Snake may experience some legal problems or the separation from a close friend or lover. Financial losses could stem from poor judgment.

The Year of the Rat—2008

An active and dramatic year for the Snake—both good and bad. Financial gains will outweigh losses, and new opportunities will present themselves.

The Year of the Ox—2009

Snakes will face obstacles and challenges to their decisions this year, although things will proceed moderately well if they quell their obstinacy.

The Year of the Tiger—2010

A year marked by many irritations, in which a Snake may be pulled into conflicts of his or her own making. The Snake must avoid senseless acts of revenge and be open to help from others.

The Year of the Rabbit—2011

A busy and moderately happy year. Numerous commitments keep the Snake occupied, and money comes and goes in equal amounts.

The Year of the Dragon—2012

A difficult year, in which the Snake will be the subject of vicious gossip from jealous associates. However the troubles will be over by summer, and with winter comes good news.

The Year of the Snake—2013

Problems in romance and business are foreseen along with the possibility of a minor bodily injury. The Snake's achievements may not match their expectations, and they must remain calm to avoid trouble.

The Year of the Horse—2014

An energetic year marked by success, although the Snake's health may be affected by problems and worries. These troubles, though, are only temporary.

The Year of the Sheep—2015

Life will be calm and leisurely, with no great gains or losses to speak of. There is the possibility of sad news at home.

The Year of the Monkey—2016

A good year. The snakes will find help where he or she needs it, although some adverse conditions and conflicts still cause anxiety.

The Year of the Rooster—2017

A most auspicious year, in which fantastic achievements and advances can be foreseen.

The Year of the Dog—2018

Opportunities present themselves and new ideas meet with approval and support, although the Snake may experience some minor health problems and could be the victim of a robbery.

Burt Bacharach, Johannes Brahms, Julie Christie, Claudette Colbert, Indira Gandhi, Greta Garbo, J. Paul Getty, Gong Li, Audrey Hepburn, Howard Hughes, Grace Kelly, John F. Kennedy, Carole King, Abraham Lincoln, Mao Tse-tung, Ferdinand Marcos, Ann Margaret, Dean Martin, Sarah Miles, Robert Mitchum, Gamal Abdel Nassar, Jacqueline Kennedy Onassis, Pablo Picasso, Edgar Allan Poe, Jean-Paul Sartre, Franz Schubert, Barbet Schroeder, Dalton Trumbo.

seven

THE HORSE

Chinese Name: Ma
Direction: South
Fixed Element: Fire
Stem: Positive
Western Sign: Gemini
Color: Black
Flower: Narcissus
Fragrance: Wildflowers
Tree: White birch
Birthstone: Topaz
Lucky number: 8
Years of the Horse: 1954, 1966, 1978, 1990, 2002, 2014

THE YEAR OF THE HORSE

A high-spirited, hectic, and adventurous year. An exhilarating time of reckless and impulsive action and risk-taking. This year people are confident, carefree, whimsical, capricious, and romantic, and everything proceeds at an energetic if not frenzied pace. Things are done on the spur of the moment. Although charged and exciting, energies are also taxed and nerves frayed by the ceaseless momentum and unpredictable shifts in the wind. Good humor and optimism, however, prevail. Old boundaries are broken, and the world's economy could experience a boom period. This is an excellent time to launch new ventures and boldly go where you have never gone before.

The film industry is said to be ruled by the Horse, and when you look at the list of famous Horses you will be surprised to see how many are outstanding successes in the movie business.

THE HORSE PERSONALITY

Those born in the Year of the Horse are energetic, unpredictable, independent, athletic, and warmly appealing. They exude a raw animal sex appeal rather than classical good looks. Impetuous and self-reliant, they are by nature restless adventurers, and seem to be always on the move. Open-minded and flexible, they can appraise a situation astutely and are expert manipulators, skillful in business as well as in love, and adept at handling money. They are extremely self-centered and can have volatile tempers; although they may forget their own explosive outbursts, others do not, for which Horses can lose respect and credibility. They can be particularly petty, petulant, and inconsiderate in satisfying their own caprices and can be forgetful and absent-minded.

Horses love action and fanfare. Although they lack both stability and perseverance, they are quick-witted and quick to act, agile in both mind and body, and as such are masters of improvisation and can juggle several acts at once while holding their own in all of them. Resentful of any limitations imposed on their freedom and nonconformists at heart, Horses will keep odd and scattered hours. When inspired, they can work for days without sleeping. They often find it hard to calm down, and the more agitated types may suffer from bouts of insomnia.

Horses cannot stand any kind of restraint, and this includes their emotions. They need to express themselves, and if forced or obliged to exercise self-inhibition will openly rebel.

Horse are not known for their constancy and perseverance. They can be extremely fickle. They fall easily in and out of love, and will most likely have many amorous liaisons before, and if, they settle down. Nonetheless, the animated, passionate, and impetuous Horse is reputed to be very susceptible to the perils of romance, and they can easily lose everything once they fall madly in love and are likely to have many affairs or marriages that end unhappily.

The female Horse will tend to take her romantic involvements lightly. Like her male counterpart, she loves to roam freely across the wide, open plain. She will either be the more placid mare or the mane-tossing nostrils-flaring firebrand, or a combination of both, but in all three cases she will be pert, saucy, occasionally skittish, and extremely nimble both physically and mentally. She requires expert handling. Her home is merely a way station where she can replenish herself before taking off again. And when she gallops away do not chase after her—that will only drive her further afield. If she is truly your Horse, she will come back to you in good time, most likely when you least expect it.

It is believed that a Horse born in the summer will lead a better life than one born in the winter. The best and most fruitful stage in the Horse's life comes in middle age, when they are mature and experienced enough to accept the shackles of responsibility. Horses of both sexes are prone to acquire wealth but not security, due to their peripatetic natures, and their offspring will most likely not benefit directly from any of the Horse's achievements.

The Chinese believe that the unbridled passions of the Horse will be greatly increased when he or she is born in the year of the Fire Horse. (The last Fire Horse year was 1966, and the next will be in 2026.) According to legend, the Fire Horse wreaks havoc wherever it goes, and many a good man has been ruined by the insatiable and uncontrolled passions of a woman born in this year. The male Fire Horse, however, is considered more fortunate, as his drive and energy may bring him distinction and acclaim.

The Horse will make the best partnerships with the Tiger, Dog, and Sheep. Dragon, Snake, Monkey, Rabbit, Boar, Rooster, or another Horse all make good secondary matches.

Horses should avoid a relationship with the Rat, who will be highly critical of their mercurial ways, and they could come into direct conflict with the stubborn and unyielding Ox, who will demand a consistency the Horse is incapable of providing.

Horse children are passionate, boisterous, mercurial, and highly energetic. They have a great love of the outdoors and require plenty of exercise, and are inclined to roam far afield, although they will always be able to find their way home, especially at mealtimes. Their restless and curious natures will keep them constantly occupied, and they will rebel against any restrictions that are placed upon them. With their adventurous spirits, they are inclined to get themselves into dangerous situations. Many Horse children are born left-handed. They are fast learners and like to get things done quickly. They also tend to be disobedient and willfully stubborn. Horse children require discipline to learn to bridle their tempers and impulsiveness.

THE FIVE TYPES OF HORSES

The Metal Horse—1930, 1990

A bold, unruly, engaging, and impetuous Horse who is highly amorous and very attractive to the opposite sex (Sean Connery is a Metal Horse). They have fine minds and keen intuition and can be highly productive. They have great powers of recuperation and an insatiable hunger for new experiences and challenges. They are also more self-centered and stubborn than Horses of other elements. When negative, they can have an irrational need for freedom and will shun close relationships out of fear of being entangled or restricted.

The Water Horse—1942, 2002

These highly nomadic individuals are cheerful, elegant, and gifted with fine business acumen. They are concerned with their own well-being and comfort, but are at the same time highly adaptable and adjust easily to change. They are good communicators and are gifted with a wonderful sense of humor. They can also be extremely fickle, changing their minds often. They are more restless than other Horses, and prone to travel and change residences frequently. When negative, they can be highly pretentious and inconsistent and demonstrate an appalling lack of consideration for others.

The Wood Horse—1954, 2014

These are more reasonable and less impatient Horses who are able to discipline their minds and think systematically. They will have happy dispositions and be highly gregarious and good conversationalists. Their interests are many and varied. They are athletic and hard-working. Progressive and unsentimental, they can easily throw out the old in order to welcome the new.

The Fire Horse—1906, 1966, 2026

The Horse's fixed element is Fire, so this is a double Fire sign; these individuals are extremely passionate, flamboyant, hot-blooded, and excitable. They have superb intellects and great personal magnetism, and rely on sheer willpower to get what they want. They are inconsistent and easily bored and require a great deal of variety in their lives. They have great flair and charm, but their many-faceted personalities along with their profusion of thoughts and feelings can make them extremely volatile. They can be skillful negotiators and problem solvers, although they are capable of being very argumentative.

The Earth Horse—1918, 1978, 2038

These Horses are slower and precise, prone to be more logical and less decisive, but also have happy and congenial dispositions. Earth makes them less abrupt and restless, able to consider all sides of a question before they act. They have good noses for investments and are more than able to bring dying businesses back to life. Their innate equine capriciousness can manifest itself over trivial things, and they can have trouble making up their minds—they can drive a waiter in a restaurant mad.

The Hours of the Rat—11 P.M. to 1 A.M.

An affectionate and companionable Horse, imbued with the Rat's talkative charm and sentimentalism, who is very good at acquiring and dealing with money.

The Hours of the Ox—1 A.M. to 3 A.M.

A more serious, reliable, and consistent Horse, who is less ruled by his or her passions and not so inclined to fall deliriously in love on the spur of the moment.

The Hours of the Tiger—3 A.M. to 5 A.M.

Alacrity and skill are expertly combined with derring-do. The Tiger is fearless although suspicious, and the Horse relies on its uncanny intuition and ability to improvise.

The Hours of the Rabbit—5 A.M. to 7 A.M.

A moderate, genteel, and debonair Horse.

The Hours of the Dragon—7 A.M. to 9 A.M.

A galloping stallion who can't stop running. A natural-born winner with a volatile temper and a tendency to overreact to everything.

The Hours of the Snake—9 A.M. to 11 A.M.

The Snake lends wisdom and discernment to the Horse, making it move more slowly but with a greater assurance of success.

The Hours of the Horse—11 A.M. to 1 P.M.

A highly energetic but graceful animal but with a skittish nature, possibly self-centered, conceited, and capricious.

The Hours of the Sheep—1 P.M. to 3 P.M.

The Sheep tames the Horse, making it a little more considerate and harmonious without quelling its fire.

The Hours of the Monkey—3 P.M. to 5 P.M.

A powerful combination of agility, swiftness, and guile. Fast movers and fast talkers, this Horse will be difficult to catch or pin down.

The Hours of the Rooster—5 P.M. to 7 P.M.

A highly perceptive Horse with a radiant disposition, blessed by the Rooster's dauntless outlook on the life.

The Hours of the Dog—7 P.M. to 9 P.M.

A more reliable, faithful, and honest Horse, who is at the same time prone to be impatient, critical, and easily agitated.

The Hours of the Boar—9 P.M. to 11 P.M.

The Boar makes the Horse more steadfast and cooperative and, at times, perhaps a little too easygoing and complacent.

THE HORSE'S PROSPECTS IN COMING YEARS

The Year of the Boar—2007

Horses could succeed academically or acquire a much sought-after job or position. A loved one may depart, or a lawsuit involving the family may arise.

The Year of the Rat—2008

A difficult year marked by money troubles and unhappy romantic entanglements. Horses must be careful to avoid confrontations, especially with the law, and refrain from lending or borrowing money.

The Year of the Ox—2009

Horses will have to work hard this year to achieve their goals, but they will be in control and some financial gains are foreseen.

The Year of the Tiger—2010

Horses will entertain a lot and accrue additional expenses. Disputes or severed relationships are possible as a result of losing their tempers.

The Year of the Rabbit—2011

This is a lucky year financially, and Horses can expect good news or new members added to their families. They will encounter few problems or obstacles.

The Year of the Dragon—2012

An unsteady and unsettling time, in which Horses are beset by worries that try their patience and cause their health to suffer. Problems, though, are not as bad as they at first seem, and the damage is not nearly as great as expected.

The Year of the Snake—2013

The Horse will experience difficulties with associates and friends, while delays are caused by unforeseen obstacles.

The Year of the Horse—2014

A prosperous year, in which plans are easily realized and recognition and advancement bring much happiness. However, Horses must be careful, as they are susceptible to contagious diseases.

The Year of the Sheep—2015

A moderate year with no serious problems but with the possibility of a change of residence or a long journey.

The Year of the Monkey—2016

A lucky year marked by unexpected gains. Horses must be wary of freak accidents and there could be some sad news, but nothing that will affect them personally.

The Year of the Rooster—2017

Good news at home, but minor problems at work could hamper progress. They could tend to be easily upset and should try to remain calm.

The Year of the Dog—2018

A good year for Horses in academic or career terms, although they may face a lawsuit or suffer from the departure of a loved one.

SOME FAMOUS HORSES

Neil Armstrong, Pearl Bailey, Ellen Barkin, Ingmar Bergman, Leonard Bernstein, Leonid Brezhnev, Michael Crichton, Sean Connery, James Dean, Lesley-Anne Down, Robert Duvall, Clint Eastwood, Robert Evans, Chris Evert, Harrison Ford, Jerry Goldsmith, Billy Graham, Ulysses S. Grant, Gene Hackman, Rita Hayworth, Patty Hearst, Werner Herzog, William Holden,

John Huston, James Earl Jones, Genghis Khan, Paul McCartney, Agnes Moorehead, Alberto Moravia, Otto Preminger, Rembrandt, Theodore Roosevelt, Roberto Rosselini, Anwar Sadat, Martin Scorsese, Sterling Silliphant, Aleksandr Solzhenistyn, Robert Stack, Joseph von Sternberg, Barbra Streisand, Raquel Welch, Anna-May Wong, Vivien Wu.

eight

THE SHEEP

Chinese Name: Yang
Direction: South-Southwest
Fixed Element: Fire
Stem: Negative
Western Sign: Cancer
Color: Light green
Flower: Narcissus
Fragrance: Apple blossom
Tree: Dogwood
Birthstone: Sapphire
Lucky Number: 12
Years of the Sheep: 1955, 1967, 1979, 1991, 2003, 2015

THE YEAR OF THE SHEEP

A calm year, in which things progress slowly but steadily. The Sheep's love of harmony promotes peaceful coexistence. During this year, people will be more sentimental, emotional, and caring toward family and loved ones. Creative ventures and the arts will flourish under the Sheep's influence. On the other hand, people can become oversensitive and nervous about minor problems and easily discouraged and hypercritical.

THE SHEEP PERSONALITY

The Sheep is nature's special child, upon whom fortune smiles, but it is also a grazing creature very much in need of a watchful and protective shepherd.

The Sheep is the most feminine sign of the Chinese zodiac, and is known for its gentle and compassionate ways. Sheep are extremely sympathetic and understanding, and generous with their time and money. Unless influenced by a more aggressive animal ruling the time of birth, they are likely to be mild-mannered and even shy. But their mettle is not to be underestimated. Beneath that subdued exterior lies an inner determination and quiet resolve, and they can respond passionately and firmly when threatened or are bent on achieving some goal. At their positive best, they are righteous, sincere, artistic, fashionable, and highly creative. At their worst, they can be intensely emotional and darkly pessimistic.

The Chinese believe that Sheep are blessed by good fortune because of their love of peace, innate kindness, and purity of heart. Theirs is the eighth sign, the number of prosperity and comfort in Chinese numerology. Thus Sheep will always have the three essentials in life—food, clothing, and shelter—and they will always find people to assist them. Others care for them a great deal, and they have fantastic luck. Things simply seem to come to them—inheritances from relatives, expensive gifts from admirers, the patronage and support of rich and powerful people. Like their friend the Rabbit, they know how to ingratiate themselves to people and are masters of the soft sell. They have great passive endurance and are always able to obtain what they want without force. They also know how to placate or evade their enemies or rally others to come to their defense.

In spite of all their luck, Sheep are fundamentally worrying pessimists liable to predict the worst. Misfortune can affect them deeply. They also find it very hard to deny themselves anything and tend to live beyond their means and have difficulty handling finances. They have expensive tastes and an inclination to overspend. They can be vague and indecisive to avoid conflict, and may be criticized for failing to take a firm stand. Their oblique approach and indirect speech can be infuriating, and they are prone to self-pity and be highly theatrical about their woes. Their moods are many and varied, and they can find it impossible to be objective.

Sheep crave love, attention, and approval. Appreciation of their talents will make them blossom spectacularly, and they can be highly creative. They understand and appreciate beauty and have discriminating tastes and a discerning eye.

The female Sheep is extremely feminine and decidedly coquettish—a real damsel or Southern belle—and is very concerned with both her costuming and personal hygiene. She is the mistress of feminine persuasion, subtly twisting arms in the most engaging, flirtatious, and cajoling manner while feigning fragility and vulnerability. She will openly show her favoritism to those she deems as special and simply ignore the unworthy or unacceptable.

Sheep need strong and loyal partners to support them. The optimistic Tiger, Horse, and Boar will readily complement them and make the best unions. Rabbit, Dragon, Snake, Rooster, or another Sheep will make good secondary matches. The Sheep will be able to find harmony with any of them.

The Rat will disapprove of the Sheep's extravagant ways and lack of self-denial, and the Sheep will not find any sympathy from the stern and unyielding Ox or the practical, no-nonsense Dog.

Sheep children are lovable little lambs who will be thoroughly petted and spoiled. Highly sensitive, they show artistic inclinations at an early age and are lovers of beauty, music, and poetry. They can be extremely dependent and needful, and find it hard to do anything for or by themselves. They hate being criticized or teased, and require loads of sympathy and understanding when their feelings are hurt. They can withdraw into a magical world of their own to insulate themselves from the cruelties of the world around them, and can harbor morbid fears that at times can even make them ill. At school or at play they seek out more dominant children to protect them. Home, security, and comfort are very important to them. They will also be extremely kind and compassionate about the suffering of others, including animals, and their affections and generosity are boundless to those they love.

THE FIVE TYPES OF SHEEP

Metal Sheep—1931, 1991

These Sheep have great faith in their own abilities and a high degree of self-worth that enables them to put up a brave front to mask their acute sensitivity and vulnerable ego. They seek beauty in all its forms and are very concerned with balance and harmony in their daily lives. Domestic and financial security are extremely important to them. They can find their emotions hard to contain, and are capable of being possessive, jealous, and overly protective of those they love.

Water Sheep—1943, 2003

These very appealing and popular Sheep have many supporters and admirers; they are also innately opportunistic. They seek out people they can depend on and often take the path of least resistance. Meek and impressionable, they will abide by the majority rule or those who have a powerful influence over them.

They mix well with people and readily absorb the ideas of others, but are fearful of change and prefer to cling to what they know. They have a tendency to feel rejected and persecuted when things do not go their way.

Wood Sheep—1955, 2015

Leisurely, good humored, thoughtful, and compassionate Sheep with high moral principles who can be overwhelmed by the misfortunes of others. As a result, they are inclined to the performance of good deeds and acts of kindness. They have complete trust in those they believe in, are sentimental, and strive to please. Money seems to always come to them from unexpected sources. They capitulate too easily when challenged, in the name of keeping the peace.

Fire Sheep—1907, 1967, 2027

These energetic and aggressive Sheep can be forthright and outspoken when challenged or offended. They are more courageous than most Sheep about following their hunches, and will take the initiative. They have an alluring personal grace and a great ability to dramatize rather than invent, making them expert peddlers of ideas—such as movie producers and agents—emphasizing strong points and glossing over weaknesses. Their emotionalism, though, can make them appear irrational. They like to entertain lavishly and can overextend their finances. When negative, they can succumb to wishful thinking and

grandiose dreams without acknowledging the benefits they have
already accumulated.

Earth Sheep—1919, 1979

These optimistic and self-reliant Sheep like to maintain a degree
of independence in spite of their strong emotional attachments.
Earth makes them conservative, cautious, responsible, and hard-
working, although, as Sheep, they will still find it difficult to
deny themselves the luxuries they regard as bare necessities. They
will go out of their way to help friends in need and can become
overly defensive and even neurotic when criticized.

INFLUENCE OF TIME OF BIRTH

The Hours of the Rat—11 P.M. to 1 A.M.

A crafty opportunist with an emotional and self-indulgent disposition, while at the same time steady and dependable.

The Hours of the Ox—1 A.M. to 3 A.M.

A reliable and conservative Sheep imbued with some of the Ox's
sturdiness and authority.

The Hours of the Tiger—3 A.M. to 5 A.M.

A temperamental and volatile Sheep; the Tiger's impetuosity
combines with the Sheep's fanciful and ingratiating ways.

The Hours of the Rabbit—5 A.M. to 7 A.M.

An unobtrusive but cunning Sheep. He or she will feign generosity and concern, but do not count on them for anything that involves personal sacrifice or inconvenience.

The Hours of the Dragon—7 A.M. to 9 A.M.

These determined Sheep are driven by the courage of their convictions and have a great need for adulation and respect.

The Hours of the Snake—9 A.M. to 11 A.M.

Self-assured, competent, secretive, and clear-headed Sheep who can make up their own minds and keep their thoughts and feelings to themselves.

The Hours of the Horse—11 A.M. to 1 P.M.

An energetic and flamboyant Sheep, with a taste for the good life, who will make money in order to spend it.

The Hours of the Monkey—3 P.M. to 5 P.M.

A self-assured Sheep who is more likely to take decisive action, and who has the Monkey's humorous and positive outlook.

The Hours of the Rooster—5 P.M. to 7 P.M.

Sheep brimming with ideas that never materialize who need others to put their talents to use.

The Hours of the Dog—7 P.M. to 9 P.M.

A more rational and sensible Sheep who is able to cope with reality and less inclined to self-pity or moroseness.

The Hours of the Boar—9 P.M. to 11 P.M.

Sympathetic Sheep who are always there when you need them and expect the same in return.

THE SHEEP'S PROSPECTS IN COMING YEARS

The Year of the Boar—2007

A year of recovery after the attacks and wounds of the Dog year. The Sheep's situation may still be somewhat tenuous or unstable. They will, however, gain access to funds that were previously withheld or unattainable.

The Year of the Rat—2008

A very good year, in which gains are foreseen from unlikely sources such as gambling. Success in business and romance.

The Year of the Ox—2009

A difficult year, marked by financial troubles, quarrels, and misunderstandings.

The Year of the Tiger—2010

Sheep will have to work hard this year to keep up with the competition. New and beneficial contacts are indicated, along with some trouble with relatives.

The Year of the Rabbit—2011

Sheep make gains financially and at work but may experience an upheaval at home; health problems may be caused by accidental injuries. Overall gains outweigh losses.

The Year of the Dragon—2012

Although Sheep are involved in numerous disputes, they face no major battles or disasters and will emerge relatively unscathed.

The Year of the Snake—2013

A year in which Sheep attain prestige and popularity. They are likely to travel and see their finances increase, although some bad news may temporarily delay their progress.

The Year of the Horse—2014

A prosperous year, with no major problems at home or at work. Sheep may suffer from a minor illness or infection.

The Year of the Sheep—2015

Surprisingly enough, this is not a particularly good year. Problems and complications mire the Sheep's plans and deplete their resources. A year to be practical and relinquish any great expectations.

The Year of the Monkey—2016
A busy and rewarding year of recognition, promotion, and personal fulfillment.

The Year of the Rooster—2017
A year marked by entertaining and expenses that tax the Sheep's bank account and cause domestic disputes and conflict. A time to be careful with finances.

The Year of the Dog—2018
A distressing time, in which Sheep have to cope with debts and romantic or family troubles. They should try to be optimistic and conservative in their behavior.

SOME FAMOUS SHEEP

Isabelle Adjani, Muhammad Ali, Miguel de Cervantes, Robert DeNiro, John Denver, Dino De Laurentis, Catherine Deneuve, Angie Dickinson, Bobby Fisher, Jennifer Jones, Michelangelo, James Michener, Rita Moreno, Leonard Nimoy, Sir Laurence Olivier, Barbara Stanwyck, Rudolph Valentino, George Wallace, Andy Warhol, John Wayne.

nine

THE MONKEY

Chinese Name: Hóu
Direction: West-Southwest
Fixed Element: Metal
Stem: Positive
Western Sign: Leo
Color: Yellow
Flower: Dandelion
Fragrance: Jasmine
Tree: Sycamore
Birthstone: Tiger eye
Lucky Number: 10
Years of the Monkey: 1956, 1968, 1980, 1992, 2004, 2016

THE YEAR OF THE MONKEY

An extremely progressive and optimistic year of gambling, improvisation, innovation, and invention, in which nothing seems impossible. "The game's afoot!" is the enthusiastic cry that resounds throughout the year. Politics, diplomacy, business, and finance are all engaged in high-stakes games of chance in which the players try to outsmart and outbluff each other. With all the excitement and activity, it will be hard to know who is winning. Stocks will soar in a frenzy of speculation and competition, and those who are quick and alert are bound to reap huge dividends. This is not a year for the timid or slow-witted, as the shrewd and cunningly playful Trickmaster Monkey sees to it that the winners find themselves laughing all the way to the bank.

THE MONKEY PERSONALITY

In the popular Chinese classic, *Journey to the West,* Sun Hóu-Tzu, the Monkey King, represents human failings that can be redeemed. The Monkey is a creature gifted with human intelligence along with man's capacity for trickery and deceit.

Monkeys are warm, buoyant, and spontaneous, often with radiant smiles and humorous and mischievous twinkles in their eyes. You cannot help but be delighted by their company, and they are expert at making themselves likable and indispensable. They are capable of great concentration and hard work, and with their superb intelligence, insightfulness, and remarkable skills they are certainly a great asset when they are on your side.

The Monkey's inimitable guile and charm are legendary in Chinese folklore. This is the sign not only of the Trickster and improviser, but of the motivator and inventor. With their keen insight, Monkeys make excellent critics. They are clever, quick-witted, innovative, highly flexible, and fast learners, able to readily absorb information and solve complex problems with ease. They can be excellent linguists. They have a wry sense of humor and a keen sense of life's ironies and contradictions.

Monkeys have lively personalities and great *joie de vivre*. They delight not only in the world around them, but un-abashedly in their own cleverness and accomplishments, and it is certainly difficult to begrudge them their childlike joy in themselves. Instinctively brilliant strategists who are supremely confident in their abilities, they are undaunted by challenge—in fact they delight in it—and are liable to be successful at what-ever they undertake. They are highly competitive and extremely good at hiding their feelings and planning their moves, able to outmaneuver their opponents with sure-footed grace and fi-nesse. They rely on skill and mental agility rather than on brute strength. Perhaps the Greek hero Odysseus, renowned for his cunning, was a Monkey. In their pursuit of money, success, and power, their prowess is unmatchable, and they are forever alert to every opportunity, which they'll instantly recognize instantly no matter how well it is hidden.

Never lie to a Monkey. Master charlatans themselves, they will see through you straight away. Oddly enough, they hold truth and objectivity in high regard. Monkeys are immensely sociable creatures, with an unshakable belief in themselves, and they will take great care to display good manners, politeness, and quiet dignity in order to ingratiate themselves to those around them.

When negative, they can be extremely vain, selfish, and egotistical, with too high an opinion of themselves, utterly self-absorbed, and totally convinced that they are smarter and wiser than everybody else. They can be actually too smart for their own good. They do not have enough respect for others, nor do they value their conquests. Because everything appears to come to Monkeys easily and effortlessly, they can have an inflated sense of their own entitlement, take people for granted, and lose interest quickly. They can also be mercenary in their outlook and behavior and are masters of revenge.

Their wily ways and clever personalities can make others suspect them and not completely trust them, and they are often misjudged or falsely accused.

Admonitions, accusations, reprimands, and insults are all simply water off a duck's back to the Monkey. They will either ignore them or find them highly amusing, the product of others' foibles, lack of insight, or spiteful jealousy of their talents and well-deserved good fortune. This does not mean that they refuse to accept criticism. Once they've had time to think about it they will do their best to rectify the situation—only don't ask them to lose face by admitting to any of it. Monkeys are always striving to improve themselves, and if things are bad they know that they can always make them better. They do have consciences and can be hit with sudden bouts of charity and generosity in the name of atonement.

Monkeys are intellectuals with acute memories and insatiable curiosity. No problem is too great for them, and if no solution is readily apparent, they will invent one. If that doesn't work, they will simply move on. Their genius is not only inventive but practical, and you won't find them wasting their time on losing propositions or in futile struggles. They are at heart realists and masters of self-preservation, who will not hesitate to take the easiest way out of an unfavorable situation. When cornered or trapped, they resort to unscrupulous means to escape.

Though they by no means lack credibility, one of the Monkey's main shortcomings is that they can yield too easily to temptation while devising means and inventing arguments to justify their actions.

The female Monkey is often a lively, stimulating, and captivating beauty who is a fashionable dresser and quite vain about her hair. She is cheerful, self-assured, efficient, resourceful, and independent, always capable of taking the initiative and acting on her own behalf. She is highly observant and calculating, and can be quite the snoop but is very guarded about her own personal affairs. You won't find her giving information away for free. She is very competitive and driven by incentives, and will work hard when she sees reason enough to do so. The Monkey woman often has very sensitive skin, and she can bruise easily or can break out in a rash when she uses too much makeup. She chooses her words carefully and is very adept at getting her way. She is a superb judge of character, and can be quite snobbish and critical.

The Monkey will make the best of all possible unions with the Dragon. The Dragon will be drawn to the Monkey's sparkle and superior wit, while the Monkey will be attracted to the Dragon's majesty and ambition. These two will never be bored with each other, and there will be mutual love and respect. The Rat likewise will seek out the Monkey for its ingenuity, and the two will share a strong affinity. Ox, Rabbit, Horse, Sheep, Rooster, Dog, and Boar will all make good secondary matches. Two Monkeys could get along fairly well if they are not too envious and competitive with each other and can learn to work together.

The Tiger and the Monkey will experience severe clashes of personality, and the Snake, with its own brand of wisdom, will be forever suspicious of the Monkey.

Monkey children are jovial, mischievous, curious, and very competitive. There are constantly driven to improve themselves, and pride themselves on their ability to acquire knowledge and learn new skills. They keep themselves busy with countless activities, and can take on several subjects at once and master them all. Ambitious and conniving, they have a selfish streak. Never content with what they have, they will regard the possessions of others with a covetous eye, while at the same time refusing to share what is theirs. When they do share, they carefully weigh what they are getting back in return. They are oblivious to any rules or restrictions placed upon them, but it is virtually impossible to be angry for very long with these clever, charming, resourceful, and bright-eyed little imps.

THE FIVE TYPES OF MONKEYS

Metal Monkey—1920, 1980

These Monkeys are very strong-willed, constant, and independent, and are driven by their need for financial security. Hardworking and very practical, they will prefer to run their own businesses, hold onto their savings, and make wise investments. They have lively dispositions and passionate and warm natures, and are ardent and demonstrative in love. Positive and very convincing, they can sell themselves to almost anyone. When negative, they can be exceedingly vain, proud, and self-centered.

Water Monkey—1932, 1992

Water imbues these Monkeys with a greater sense of purpose and cooperation, and they are able to motivate others with their flair and originality. Both proficient and patient in the pursuit of their goals, they understand the art of compromise and know how to work around obstacles rather than waste time and energy trying to overcome them. They are always able to present things in the best possible light, and as a result their ideas meet with little resistance. They have secretive but kind natures, but are also likely to be more easily offended than Monkeys of other elements. When negative, they can be indecisive, evasive, and erratic.

Wood Monkey—1994, 2004

These are restless Monkeys with pioneering spirits, who are always on the lookout for greener pastures. They leap at new challenges and do not take setbacks lightly. They maintain high standards and are constantly searching for answers and striving to elevate themselves above their present situations. They are highly intuitive and keenly aware of everything that is going on around them, with uncanny ability to foresee the course events. Ordered and resourceful, they are rarely given to exaggeration or speculation.

Fire Monkey—1956, 2016

These are the most forceful of all the Monkeys. Self-assured and determined, Fire Monkeys are expressive and truthful with their emotions and have a keen interest in the opposite sex. They have great vitality and fertile imaginations. They are ultra-competitive and very ambitious and will strive to be the top in their professions. They can also be exceedingly jealous and suspicious that others are deceiving them. They are lucky in speculative ventures and relish power and control. When negative, they can be stubborn, opinionated, and very argumentative.

Earth Monkey—1908, 1968, 2028

A reliable Monkey with a warm but calm and collected nature. Earth Monkeys value their integrity and are honest and straightforward. They are likely to be well-read intellectuals or academically inclined. They are genuinely kind and loving to those they care for and given to performing selfless acts of charity. They are conscientious and capable of achieving distinction as a result of their thoroughness and devotion to duty.

INFLUENCE OF TIME OF BIRTH

The Hours of the Rat—11 P.M. to 1 A.M.

This effervescent and charming Monkey savors life's cornucopia while hanging on to his or her money.

The Hours of the Ox—1 A.M. to 3 A.M.

A more rigid and straight-laced Monkey who is less inclined to trickery and cajolery.

The Hours of the Tiger—3 A.M. to 5 A.M.

An exuberant, self-confident, and impulsive Monkey who is wary of others and unwilling to take advice or accept defeat.

The Hours of the Rabbit—5 A.M. to 7 A.M.

A less mischievous and far more cautious and restrained type of Monkey, who is highly intuitive in dealing with and assessing others, often uncannily so.

The Hours of the Dragon—7 A.M. to 9 A.M.

Highly ambitious and driven, this Monkey takes on more than he or she can handle.

The Hours of the Snake—9 A.M. to 11 A.M.

An elusive and secretive Monkey who is a master escape artist, gifted with a penetrating intellect and almost psychic powers.

The Hours of the Horse—11 A.M. to 1 P.M.

This highly capricious individual lacks perseverance and trustworthiness and plays entirely by his or her own rules.

The Hours of the Sheep—1 P.M. to 3 P.M.

A romantic dreamer with an acquiescent nature, but also conniving and opportunistic.

The Hours of the Monkey—3 P.M. to 5 P.M.

The "double" or "pure" Monkey will be supremely optimistic, charming, convivial and very quick on his or her feet. The ultimate Tricksters, they can get away with murder.

The Hours of the Rooster—5 P.M. to 7 P.M.

This adventurous, colorful, and unconventional individual is quite capable of realizing high aspirations.

The Hours of the Dog—7 P.M. to 9 P.M.

A Monkey who is emotionally detached, but with a wry and satirical sense of humor coupled with a strong sense of reality.

The Hours of the Boar—9 P.M. to 11 P.M.

This far less secretive or deceitful Monkey can be relied on to keep his or her word and uphold their end of the deal.

THE MONKEY'S PROSPECTS IN COMING YEARS

The Year of the Boar—2007

Monkeys will be faced with business disputes and financial or legal troubles. Problems will be solved but only after much compromising. Monkeys will have to make some difficult concessions and even tolerate the insults of enemies. This is a year in which they should trust no one, including their best friends.

The Year of the Rat—2008

A lucky and prosperous year, in which money comes from unexpected sources and new members are added to the Monkey's family.

The Year of the Ox—2009

Pleasures and profits are limited this year, and the loss of some personal belongings is indicated. Family life runs smoothly, but the Monkey may be forced to travel or suffer from some chronic illness.

The Year of the Tiger—2010

The Monkey is very vulnerable this year and may be forced to flee, travel, or borrow money. A year to lie low and wait.

The Year of the Rabbit—2011

A good year, as tranquillity is restored at home and at work and new opportunities present themselves. The Monkey receives help from unlikely sources, although gains will be modest.

The Year of the Dragon—2012

Troubles and unsettled differences could be a source of distraction this year. Monkeys may have to spend their own money to implement their plans. Gains are made in knowledge or technical skills that can be put to later use.

The Year of the Snake—2013

Monkeys receive assistance and support from friends and superiors. Good times are indicated, although there could be some domestic disputes. Monkeys should avoid confrontations at all costs.

The Year of the Horse—2014

Monkeys are beset by frustrations and worries this year, but their problems will work themselves out if they are acquiescent and remain calm and lower their expectations.

The Year of the Sheep—2015

A busy year in which money is easily made, although Monkeys are faced with unforeseen expenses. They will benefit from meeting new and powerful people and will have to travel or entertain more than usual. Some minor illness or domestic unhappiness is indicated.

The Year of the Monkey—2016

An excellent year, in which Monkeys will make fantastic progress. Achievement, recognition, and happiness are all indicated. With all this excitement and optimism, Monkeys must be careful not to overexert themselves.

The Year of the Rooster—2017

A stable and moderate year, in which Monkeys will have the resources they need to push their plans through. Home life could be neglected due to too many commitments, and Monkeys must be careful not to overextend themselves or underestimate the opposition.

The Year of the Dog—2018

A difficult year, marked by disappointments. People break their promises and plans go askew. Monkey could suffer losses in their investments and should not lend money.

SOME FAMOUS MONKEYS

Milton Berle, Jacqueline Bisset, Montgomery Clift, Bette Davis, Charles Dickens, Michael Douglas, Frederico Fellini, Paul Gauguin, Mel Gibson, Rex Harrison, Mick Jagger, Lyndon Johnson, Edward Kennedy, David Lean, Leonardo da Vinci, Walter Matthau, Toshiro Mifune, John Milton, Maureen O'Hara, Peter O'Toole, Valerie Perrine, Nelson Rockefeller, Eleanor Roosevelt, Omar Sharif, James Stewart, Gene Tierney, Francois Truffaut, Harry Truman, Bai Yang, Andrew Young.

ten

THE ROOSTER

Chinese Name: Ji
Direction: West
Fixed Element: Metal
Stem: Negative
Western Sign: Virgo
Color: Violet
Flower: Chrysanthemum
Fragrance: Myrrh
Tree: Oak
Birthstone: Topaz
Lucky Number: 6
Years of the Rooster: 1957, 1969, 1981, 1993, 2005, 2017

THE YEAR OF THE ROOSTER

A buoyant and optimistic year, but also precariously balanced, for the colorful Rooster is prone to nonsensical schemes and to flaunting its authority, which can set off an endless number of petty disputes. People tend to be ostentatious and self-conscious about their image and dissension and debates on all fronts come about as a result of the Rooster's proclivity for argument. There is much loud talk for talk's sake that seems to go nowhere, and people are prone to take offense at the smallest slight. Simple things are made to appear complicated, and people find themselves expending maximum effort for minimum return. However, there are no real confrontations or damage done. This is a year to be practical and conservative and refrain from speculative ventures, then we will get by without real hardship.

THE ROOSTER PERSONALITY

Quixotic and eccentric, the Rooster is possibly the most misunderstood sign of the Chinese zodiac. Outwardly colorful and self-assured, they are at heart traditional and conservative. The Rooster-born, especially the men, will tend to be attractive and often dashingly handsome. Roosters strut about with preening dignity, and even the shyest of this group can be distinguished by their fine feathers and regal bearing. There are two distinct types of Rooster: those who are extremely talkative and those who are solemn, withdrawn, and observant. All Roosters are neat, upright, decisive, organized, alert, and very direct. They love to argue and debate, and can be extremely critical, demonstrating an appalling lack of discretion and little regard for the feelings of others. They can also be completely blind to their own faults, and when criticized by others are unable to take their own medicine.

Adept at expressing themselves in both speech and writing, Roosters love to show how knowledgeable they are and recount their adventures and accomplishments. If you join one of them in a debate, be prepared for a long argument that may leave you exhausted. For all their braggadocio, however, Roosters are not nearly as self-assured as they appear. They are constantly in need of affirmation and are therefore highly susceptible to flattery and their own delusions of grandeur. When negative, they can be egoistic, vain, harshly opinionated, and abrasive.

They are very adroit at handling money and are natural experts in accounting, budgeting, and organization. If owed money, Roosters will collect. In fact, Roosters are masters of efficiency who love taking on difficult assignments and demonstrating their expertise.

All Roosters are perfectionists and tireless workers. They have a keen eye for detail, but are also prone to intellectual or theoretical flights of fancy that make their ideas simply inapplicable in any real or human terms. Their dreams are often farfetched and overambitious, and, as a result, they are bound to experience many disappointments in life. They must learn to come down to earth and realize that it is not their cock-crow that makes the sun rise. They are, however, extremely brave and dauntless under duress, sincere in their desire to help others, and generally well-meaning in their endeavors.

A Rooster born at dawn will be the loudest and most talkative of the lot, while those born at night are the exact opposite—serious, self-contained, even withdrawn and uncommunicative.

Roosters love to attract attention. They will dress sharply and have a tendency to overdecorate their homes or offices. They are extremely impressed by medals, awards, and honorary titles of all kinds, and will do their best to collect some of their own. Meticulous and competent, with strong administrative abilities, a natural passion for work, and a driving will to succeed, most Roosters will be successful early in life. Optimistic and dauntless, they will never change their course of action once they have set themselves upon it, no matter what people say or even if they are in reality charging windmills. Like Don Quixote, they insist on dreaming the impossible dream. Ironically enough, some of their grandiose schemes do work out, and many millionaires are born in the Year of the Rooster. Roosters are always able to find money, often in the most common or mundane places. According to a Chinese saying, "Chickens can always find food, even in the hardest ground."

The female Rooster, or Hen, will tend to be more down to earth and far less pretentious and ambitious than her male counterpart. She is also more adaptable and fares far better in social situations. She is extremely efficient and hardworking and has a tremendous amount of energy. Routine appeals to her, and she is highly capable and productive. Dutiful and careful, she could excel in any work requiring concentration and precision, as well as making a patient and thorough teacher, a watchful and protective mother, or an attentive and solicitous wife. Precise and orderly, with an arsenal of remedies for every illness and a detailed list of things to do, she can be helpful and nurturing to the extreme, with a tendency to harp on issues while reminding you what is next on her busy schedule. This is because she cares and is there to help. She takes her responsibilities seriously and enjoys the power and authority that they confer.

Roosters will make the best match with the wise and venerable Snake or the sturdy and down-to-earth Ox. They will both love the brightness of the Rooster's disposition and dauntless outlook on life. Dragons will find both the Rooster's directness and grandiose schemes very much to their liking, and will appreciate the Rooster's outgoing energy and ambition. Tiger, Sheep, Monkey, and Boar make good secondary matches.

The Rooster will not find harmony with the sensitive and peace-loving Rabbit, who will be utterly offended by the Rooster's glaring directness, lack of discretion, and harsh criticism. The Rat will find the Rooster arrogant and aloof, and the two will come into direct conflict. The Dog will disapprove of and even resent the Rooster's strutting ways and flights of fancy.

Rooster children will be neat and orderly, intelligent and precise, good students and fast learners. Their parents will find them very demanding, but also dependable and self-disciplined.

Tough and independent, they are not always crying for help. They will be amazingly discerning critics and very straightforward and factual about voicing their opinions. Their minds are pure and they loathe hypocrisy, and will be the first to point out any inconsistencies or flaws in your behavior. They will be astonished and confused if you get angry at them. They were, after all, simply telling you the truth.

THE FIVE TYPES OF ROOSTERS

Metal Rooster—1921, 1981

These opinionated and headstrong Roosters have an overriding need for recognition and fame. They are also very practical and industrious and could dazzle others with their brilliant powers of deduction. They may be overly fastidious about their personal image and overly concerned with order and hygiene in their environment. They are gifted and high-powered orators, inclined to simply shout down their opponents. Although concerned with material wealth, they find fulfillment in service to humanity and may be passionately committed to instituting social reforms for the good of all.

Water Rooster—1933, 1993

A more reasonable type of Rooster given to clear thinking and practicality and able to recognize an impossible situation or insurmountable obstacle. They have tremendous energy and initiative and are proficient writers and speakers, able to inspire action in others to expedite their progress. They are intellectuals with a love of culture, and they will also have very strong scientific leanings. When negative they can be overly obsessed with perfection and procedures, making them bureaucratic and mired in trivialities.

Wood Rooster—1945, 2005

A much less stubborn and opinionated Rooster who is more considerate of others and has a wider outlook on life. Nonetheless, being Roosters, they still have a tendency to complicate matters, be overly regimental, and harsh-tongued when crossed. Wood makes them progress-oriented, and with the Rooster's virtues of integrity and honesty they will be excellent performers in whatever they do. Open-minded and fair, they are capable of giving unselfishly of themselves for the welfare of others.

Fire Rooster—1957, 2017

Extremely vigorous and highly motivated, these are Roosters of strong principles who are utterly singleminded in their pursuit of success. Fanatical about their beliefs, they can be inflexible and highly temperamental and overdramatic, but they are totally ethical and professional in their dealings with others. They have very strong managerial and leadership abilities and could project quite a dynamic and authoritative public image.

Earth Rooster—1909, 1969, 2029

These efficient, analytical, accurate, and probing Roosters dig deep for the truth, are judicious about their work, and are extremely systematic. They can cut through the brambles and get to the plain and simple facts. They are undaunted by responsibility and can be dogmatic and missionary in their zeal. Hard taskmasters and critics, they are tireless workers who will reap the rewards of their efforts if their goals are practical.

INFLUENCE OF TIME OF BIRTH

The Hours of the Rat—11 P.M. to 1 A.M.

A Rooster imbued with the Rat's charm, curiosity, and conviviality. Still argumentative but with decisively more pleasant manners.

The Hours of the Ox—1 A.M. to 3 A.M.

A more down-to-earth Rooster but harsh and heavy-handed when put in a position of authority.

The Hours of the Tiger—3 A.M to 5 A.M.

An impulsive, supremely overconfident, and at times incoherent Rooster who can be highly excitable and changeable.

The Hours of the Rabbit—5 A.M. to 7 A.M.

Quiet and efficient, with an element of the Rabbit's cunning, and less likely to be harsh or troublesome.

The Hours of the Dragon—7 A.M. to 9 A.M.

A fastidious, assertive, and fearless Rooster who will plow through the opposition and refuse to relinquish power.

The Hours of the Snake—9 A.M. to 11 A.M.

A considerably more detached and secretive Rooster who may even have a certain amount of discretion when it comes to voicing personal opinions.

The Hours of the Horse—11 A.M. to 1 P.M.

A flamboyant and colorful but more practical and agile Rooster with sharp reflexes and the ability to implement plans that can actually reap high dividends.

The Hours of the Sheep—1 P.M. to 3 P.M.

A less assertive and egotistical Rooster who may have a touch of the Sheep's coy bashfulness and more refined and considerate ways.

The Hours of the Monkey—3 P.M. to 5 P.M.

A crafty, alert, and congenial Rooster who is purposeful and adept at making deals and does't take him- or herself so seriously.

The Hours of the Rooster—5 P.M. to 7 P.M.

A "double" or "pure" Rooster whose fastidiousness, obsessive efficiency, and harsh criticism may be too much for most people to tolerate.

The Hours of the Dog—7 P.M. to 9 P.M.

A fair-minded, idealistic, and less opinionated but calculating Rooster who could be prone to bouts of erratic or cantankerous behavior. Both the Rooster and the Dog are known for their sharp tongues.

The Hours of the Boar—9 P.M. to 11 P.M.

A more sensual, generous, and unselfish Rooster who is incapable of dishonesty and who will insist on helping you whether you want it or not.

THE ROOSTER'S PROSPECTS IN COMING YEARS

The Year of the Boar—2007

Roosters are plagued by unexpected difficulties, hindrances, and setbacks and they must not be misled by so-called good news or the advice of friends but be wary and prudent.

The Year of the Rat—2008

A difficult year in which money is hard to come by and the Rooster finds little to no assistance from friends or associates. Troubles at home and minor health problems are indicated as the Rooster must go it alone to solve his problems.

The Year of the Ox—2009

A good year in which the Rooster regains lost power and receives assistance from friends. Loss of blood is indicated this year, and the Rooster must be careful to avoid injury from sharp objects.

The Year of the Tiger—2010

A fruitful year where business and money are concerned. Things go according to plan although the Rooster may face some worries or troubles at home.

The Year of the Rabbit—2011

Roosters could lose money this year as they are prone to miscalculations. This is not a time to try and act independently but seek the support and assistance of others.

The Year of the Dragon—2012

A prosperous year marked by gains and success. A birth or a marriage within the family are highly probable.

The Year of the Snake—2013

No large monetary gains are foreseen this year, but Roosters are able to maintain their position and diminish any losses or expenses. There is the possibility of being the victim of freak accidents or malicious gossip.

The Year of the Horse—2014

The Rooster encounters many obstacles this year and will be forced to make unwilling compromises. Although the work is beset by quarrels and disputes, there is good news regarding family.

The Year of the Sheep—2015

The Rooster receives good news and advancement in career and life is quieter and more settled.

The Year of the Monkey—2016

Financial problems, business failure, or personal suffering of some kind are possible this year. A year for Roosters to be cautious and investigate everything thoroughly, as they are prone to make errors in judgment.

The Year of the Rooster—2017

Problems are solved with ease and the Rooster makes a magnificent comeback after the difficult Year of the Monkey.

Although gains will only moderate this year losses will be minimal. Plans go smoothly but there may be some unhappiness or frustration in the Rooster's personal life.

SOME FAMOUS ROOSTERS

Albert R. Broccoli, Grover Cleveland, Alexander Dubcek, Paul Gallico, Andrei Gromyko, Alex Haley, Katherine Hepburn, Elton John, Elia Kazan, Deborah Kerr, Jayne Mansfield, Yves Montand, Pope Paul IV, Jane Russell, Jessica Tandy, Peter Ustinov, Rachel Ward.

eleven

THE DOG

Chinese Name: Gou
Direction: West-Northwest
Fixed Element: Metal
Stem: Positive
Western Sign: Libra
Color: Turquoise
Flower: Calendula
Fragrance: Balsam
Tree: Cherry
Birthstone: Ruby
Lucky Number: 9
Years of the Dog: 1958, 1970, 1982, 1994, 2006, 2018

THE YEAR OF THE DOG

This is, in a sense, the year of the underdog. Liberty and equality are staunchly advocated by the Dog, whose sense of justice and fair play lead to major confrontations and dissent, with the weaker parties emerging victorious. Controversial issues are addressed, and changes instigated. People are less materialistic and more idealistic in their outlook and prone to performing charitable acts and championing worthy causes. The Dog's resoluteness brings about clashes, upheavals, and rebellions against tyranny and oppression, but the Dog's good sense and largesse also ensures that peace and stability are reinstated once the necessary reforms have been made.

This can be a worrying year, but with the Dog on guard there is actually no real cause for alarm. The Chinese, though, fear the Year of the Metal Dog, which is said to bring war and calamity.

THE DOG PERSONALITY

People born in the Year of the Dog are warm, idealistic, honest, straightforward, and intelligent, with a deep sense of loyalty and a passion for justice and fair play. Often they protect the interests of others more avidly than their own. They are amiable, animated, and unpretentious, and exude a strong sexual appeal. Egalitarian and democratic, they will listen to reason and know how to get along well with others and meet them halfway. They have a noble and altruistic character and a strong sense of duty. People trust them and hold them in high esteem, making them good although often reluctant leaders.

Often Dogs will be born into a good family. If they aren't, they will manage to elevate their status in life without denying their families or concealing their origins.

Dogs can be prone to bouts of erratic and cantankerous behavior in which little things seem to irritate them tremendously. Inclined to pessimism and a certain degree of paranoia, they expect trouble where there is none and can worry unnecessarily. However, their predictions do occasionally come true, as Dogs have a natural guardian instinct for immediately spotting a friend or foe, the good and the bad. They also have a tendency to categorize people according to these distinctions. In the Dog's mind there are no gray areas. You are either with them or against them, an ally or an enemy. Their decision to trust or not trust you will be a final one. If you are among the chosen few, then you are indeed fortunate, as the Dog is an immensely loyal friend and ally who will not hesitate to come to your aid or defense. And as much as they are loyal, they expect the same in return. Besides injustice, disloyalty and cowardice are the things they despise the most.

Although they can at times be pugnacious and quarrelsome, Dogs rarely if ever resort to underhanded means to win a fight. They fight their battles in the open, meeting the enemy face to face. But generally speaking, Dogs only attack when challenged on their home ground. While genuinely warm and generous with their friends, they can be critical of and cold to the people they dislike. Practical and very realistic, they are fearless and outspoken and can have a razor sharp tongue. When negative they can be belligerent, argumentative, rigidly opinionated, and extremely cynical and caustic. If hurt or taken advantage of, they can retaliate fiercely and without mercy.

The female Dog often has a warm and lasting beauty. Brigitte Bardot and Sophia Loren are examples of her glamorous and enduring appeal. She forms her friendships slowly, getting to know you a little a time, sounding you out while she sees if you meet with her approval and possess the qualities she deems appropriate to form a loyal and lasting friendship. She can be abrupt and impatient when crossed, but on the whole she is caring and attentive to the needs of others. Her husband and children will find her a friend and ally who is cooperative and unbiased and who is neither possessive nor interfering. She will enjoy outdoor activities such as swimming, hiking, and tennis, and will love to dance and attend parties.

Dogs will be most compatible with the Tiger and the Horse. Rat, Rabbit, Snake, Monkey, Boar, or another Dog make good secondary matches. The Rooster and the Dog will have difficulty understanding one another, and the Dog will not be able to tolerate the indecisive and self-indulgent Sheep, who will find the Dog callous and insensitive. Dragon and Dog will come into direct conflict, as the Dog will be highly critical of the Dragon and the Dragon will be enraged by the Dog's derision of his grand schemes.

Dog children have cheerful and harmonious dispositions. Natural-born realists, they expect little of others and accept their parents for who and what they are. They have a keen sense of humor and an amazing clarity of perception and are forthright and candid. Confident and loyal, they know how to stand up for themselves and are very protective of other family members. They are reasonable and cooperative when asked to help around the house, and although they insist on a certain degree of independence, they will stay close to home. When offended or hurt they can become belligerent and rebellious, but their anger subsides quickly and they will regain their reason and inner equilibrium.

THE FIVE TYPES OF DOGS

Metal Dog—1910, 1970, 2030

Metal is the Dog's fixed element, so this is a double Metal sign. The Tibetans call this particular combination the "Iron Dog" and regard it apprehensively. It will either be very good or very bad.

These Dogs will be unswerving in their convictions and can devote their lives selflessly to whatever cause they choose to take on. Stern and principled, their loyalty will be unquestionable and they will have strong political views. They take matters very seriously, especially when they concern the affairs of their own hearts or their loyalty to their country. Never indecisive, they will choose a side and stick with it and can resort to extreme measures in the name of their convictions and loyalties. They can be ruthless when attacked and hell-bent on the annihilation of their enemies.

Water Dog—1922, 1982, 2042

A highly intuitive type of Dog who will be difficult to deceive and who has a more reflective and sympathetic nature. They will have a tendency to be lenient with themselves as well as others and are prone to indulging in wild sprees and other acts of self-gratification. They are nonetheless able to contain their emotions beneath a calm and very charming demeanor. Good listeners and sound counselors, they are fluid in their expression and fated to be surrounded by many friends and admirers. The female Water Dog is often a striking and alluring beauty. Ava Gardner is an outstanding example of the Water Dog in all her glory.

Wood Dog—1934, 1994

These gregarious, charming, and warmhearted Dogs will form close and lasting relationships in spite of their fundamental wariness of others. Although attracted to money and success, they will not be overtly materialistic and will seek intellectual stimulation and work hard to improve and develop themselves.

They have refined tastes and are socially graceful with a strong aptitude for dealing with large numbers of people from various walks of life. Energetic, cooperative, and very popular, the Wood Dog is happiest when involved in a partnership or some powerful affiliation.

Fire Dog—1946, 2006

A dramatic and charismatic Dog with great magnetic charm who will be very attractive to the opposite sex. Independent and courageous, they are creative and pure in their expression and not at all afraid of getting involved with others. They can be defiant and openly rebellious when forced to act against their will, and are constantly seeking new adventures and experiences. They are very fierce when attacked and will not make threats that they cannot carry out. With their driving willpower, honesty, faith, and idealism they are able to overcome obstacles and succeed in great and daring endeavors.

Earth Dog—1958, 2018

These practical, secretive, quiet, and less sentimental Dogs value their individuality and self-respect. They move slowly but purposefully and seldom deviate from their fixed scale of values. Good fighters and survivors, they are realists who are never completely subdued by defeat or blinded by victory. They are prone to be overachievers who demand extreme loyalty and dedication from others.

The Hours of the Rat—11 P.M. to 1 A.M.

A loving but not so generous Dog who is careful with money.

The Hours of the Ox—1 A.M. to 3 A.M.

A blunt and plain-spoken Dog, conservative and austere, whose honesty and truthfulness are unquestionable.

The Hours of the Tiger—3 A.M. to 5 A.M.

Energetic, passionate, and courageous, this Dog could be even more impatient and critical than most.

The Hours of the Rabbit—5 A.M. to 7 A.M.

A peace-loving Dog who will also carefully consider the pros and cons before choosing sides.

The Hours of the Dragon—7 A.M. to 9 A.M.

A dogmatic idealist with high moral standards and aspirations who could achieve much.

The Hours of the Snake—9 A.M. to 11 A.M.

These more silent and brooding Dogs are not adverse to compromising their sense of justice and fair play to attain their goals.

The Hours of the Horse—11 A.M. to 1 P.M.

An alert, nimble Dog with lightning responses and a sunny and friendly disposition who will blithely move on if you are too imposing or demanding.

The Hours of the Sheep—1 P.M. to 3 P.M.

A kind-hearted and sympathetic and less critical Dog, artistic and pessimistic, with a keen sense of fair play.

The Hours of the Monkey—3 P.M. to 5 P.M.

Character and ingenuity come together to form a sparkling and amusing Dog with a lively wit and a pliable conscience.

The Hours of the Rooster—5 P.M. to 7 P.M.

These Dogs are very competent and analytical but prone to preaching, and preaching they do ad infinitum without ever seeming to get to the point.

The Hours of the Dog—7 P.M. to 9 P.M.

Open-hearted Dogs with honest natures, forever alert and defending their territory while looking for wrongs to right, souls to save, and just causes to fight for.

The Hours of the Boar—9 P.M. to 11 P.M.

These sensuous and emotionally driven Dogs will take the critical moral high ground with others while refusing to deny their own indulgences.

The Year of the Boar—2007

Some gains through speculations or investments are possible, but Dogs will be faced with delays and additional expenses that diminish their overall profits. Dogs could cultivate new and influential friends and make new contacts.

The Year of the Rat—2008

A good year for the Dog, marked by business successes or profits from investments. The Dog could experience some domestic problems—possibly with children—and should refrain from lending money.

The Year of the Ox—2009

A year of uncertainties and misunderstandings, in which Dogs must avoid confrontations and making hasty decisions. They may have to make some difficult concessions or be faced with additional expenses.

The Year of the Tiger—2010

A moderately happy year, with no serious disputes. Dogs will be faced with some romantic quarrels or troubles but they will ultimately be inconsequential. Net results will be mixed, and family and friends will make excessive demands on their time and energy.

The Year of the Rabbit—2011

A good year for Dogs to go into business or launch a new venture. Problems will be solved with minimum effort and few complications.

The Year of the Dragon—2012

A difficult year, in which Dogs will be constantly at war with the competition, and people tend to take advantage of their weak position. They could also be susceptible to infections. Good news comes with the winter.

The Year of the Snake—2013

A very good year. Although they may have to work hard, Dogs will receive due recognition and rewards for their efforts and will benefit greatly from the advice and support of friends and associates.

The Year of the Horse—2014

An expansive and progressive year marked by promotions and financial gains. However, there is the possibility of unhappy news at home or the loss of some personal belonging.

The Year of the Sheep—2015

Dogs are hounded by anxiety and worries this year, but they can prevent losses and resolve conflicts if they are patient and careful with their words.

The Year of the Monkey—2016

A hectic and busy year, but not nearly as fruitful as it first appears. Extra expenditures, travel, or a change of residence are indicated. There will be good news at home, and the Dog will attract new and important people.

The Year of the Rooster—2017

Health and romantic problems beset the Dog this year, and there could also be trouble with superiors or the government. Friends are not particularly sympathetic or helpful, and Dogs find it hard to collect money owed to them.

The Year of the Dog—2018

A quiet and protected year in which the Dog will see some advances in career but with no significantly large profits or returns.

SOME FAMOUS DOGS

James Agee, Brigitte Bardot, Charles Bronson, Carol Burnett, Pierre Cardin, Cher, Chou En-lai, Bill Clinton, Sir Winston Churchill, Ava Gardner, Herbert Hoover, Sophia Loren, Norman Mailer, Golda Meir, Liza Minnelli, Ralph Nader, David Niven, Elvis Presley, Itzhak Rabin, Oliver Stone, François-Marie de Voltaire.

twelve

THE BOAR

Chinese Name: Zhu
Direction: North-Northwest
Fixed Element: Water
Stem: Negative
Western Sign: Scorpio
Color: Purple
Flower: Calla lily
Fragrance: Ambergris
Tree: Acacia
Birthstone: Moonstone
Lucky Number: 5
Years of the Boar: 1947, 1959, 1971, 1983, 1995, 2007, 2019

THE YEAR OF THE BOAR

A year of plenty and good will for all, imbued with a feeling
of abundance, contentment and security. People make new
friends and entertain a lot, and are involved in charitable and
social functions. Business and industry thrive, but, given the

Boar's indecisive nature, people hesitate to take full advantage of the time. The tolerant, sensual, and indulgent Boar fills everyone with a sense of well-being, extravagance, generosity, and chivalry. Life is for living, and living well. People may also find themselves regretting impulsive acts of generosity. A year to be wary of excess and exercise prudence in money matters.

THE BOAR PERSONALITY

Boars are known for their honesty, simplicity, and perseverance. Like the Rabbit and the Sheep, they seek peace and harmony in their existence. Physically strong, courageous, sensual, and gallant, they can apply themselves wholeheartedly to their work and be relied upon to bring whatever they start to completion. With their bountiful supply of energy, they will work hard and play hard. Considerate, generous, and loyal, they make lasting friendships and enjoy social gatherings of all kinds. They love to throw parties and entertain, and wallow gloriously in the company of friends and loved ones. When negative, their wanton pursuit of pleasure can lead to debauchery and even depravity. Unable to contain their enormous appetites, they can be easily corrupted and debased by those who know how to exploit their weaknesses.

The genial Boar is completely trustworthy. They rarely possesses ulterior motives and at times can be too innocent and naive, making it easy for others to take advantage of them. However, fortune tends to favor them because of their honest, kind, and giving natures. Although quick-tempered, they hate conflict of any kind and will do their best to placate or accommodate their opponents. As friends, they will be there to help when you need it the most, and whatever you do for them they will be sure to pay you back doubly. Although materialistic by nature, they love to share what they have, taking genuine pleasure in seeing others enjoy the bounty of their labors. They are virtually defenseless against deception, and as a result are often easily parted from their money.

They are amorous and sensuous creatures driven by strong passions, and have extraordinary vigor and stamina. When they love, they love with their whole heart and do not know how to conceal their emotions. As a result, they are often hurt, and the wound can last for years. On the other hand, they can be incredibly thick-skinned—the Boar has a tough hide—and can dismiss insults, accusations, and other unpleasantness with a laugh or casual shrug and go about their business. However, when pushed too far they can respond with savage power and be formidable opponents.

Because of their inability to say "No" to themselves as well as to their friends and family, Boars are likely to experience bankruptcy or its near equivalent at least once in their lives, but they have remarkable powers of recuperation and always manage to make brilliant comebacks. They never seem to take calamity too seriously. The secret of their success lies in their dauntless faith, courage, generosity, and resilience.

The female Boar is very personable and modest. Although she loves with complete abandonment, she will tend to do it quietly and even secretly, worshiping someone from a distance with passionate devotion without the person knowing it. She will devote all of her energy to the ones she loves and demand little in return. She is extremely trusting and remarkably pure in her expression. Like all Boars, she will be either incredibly clean and neat or very untidy.

Boars make the best unions with the Rabbit or the Sheep. Rat, Ox, Tiger, Dragon, Horse, Rooster and Dog all make good secondary matches. Two Boars together are likely to find each other too similar and boring. Boars should avoid both the Snake and the Monkey. The honest and simple Boar will be no match for their cunning and guile. With the Snake, especially, the Boar will experience deep animosity and lasting conflict.

Boar children are dependable, self-reliant, and determined. Physically strong, they are able to cope with pain and suffering without complaining, and they are courageous in the face ad-versity. They are not easily discouraged or depressed. They have passionate natures, and it is virtually impossible for them to be detached or casual in their affections. If they love their parents, they will worship the ground they walk on; if not, they will re-proach themselves for their lack of devotion. They will require little attention, although they must feel assured that the support they need is there when required. They can take reproach in stride, and setbacks only instill them with renewed vigor. Boar children put their complete strength and dedication into any of their undertakings. They are utterly blind to any faults in those they love and are intensely loyal to their friends.

THE FIVE TYPES OF BOARS

Metal Boar—1911, 1971, 2051

These Boars are proud and passionate, with excessive appetites and overwhelming sentiments. Intense and domineering, they are very extroverted and sociable. Openly demonstrative with their affections, direct and trusting, they can overestimate their friends and underestimate their foes. Forceful and highly ambitious, with immense powers of endurance, they will not concede defeat without a fight and can be violent in their anger and be dangerous enemies.

Water Boar—1923, 1983

Diplomatic, cordial, peaceful, and perceptive, Water Boars understand people's secret desires and are adroit at bargaining with their opponents. They always look for the best in people, often refusing to recognize or believe in evil intentions, and have a deep faith in their own beliefs and in their loved ones.

They are highly gregarious and given to strong and passionate outpourings of love and affection. When negative, they can be obsessed with sex and prone to excessive drink and other sensual indulges at the expense of others.

Wood Boar—1935, 1995

Although expert manipulators of people for personal gain, Wood Boars are nonetheless extremely kind-hearted and love to help others and get along with everyone. Great promoters and persuasive talkers, they are adept at getting financing for their business deals and will take on ambitious ventures. They love to entertain and bring people together, but can be indiscriminate about whom they associate with.

Fire Boar—1947, 2007

Fire Boars are courageous and driven by powerful emotions. They are intrepid and optimistic, believing entirely in their own abilities, have no fear of the unknown, and will try their hand at almost anything and succeed against overwhelming odds. They are extremely energetic and very sensual. They are motivated by love and will accumulate wealth in order to provide for those they care for. They are extremely generous, even to strangers. These Boars will prefer manufacturing or labor-oriented enterprises such as building and construction, as they enjoy employing large numbers of people. They are always able gather people around them to participate in both their virtues and their vices. When negative, they can be stubborn, willful, and bullying, but generally they have great largesse and are decidedly unprejudiced.

Earth Boar—1959, 2019

Earth Boars possess great willpower and patience and will steadfastly work toward a goal until they attain it, with an extraordinary capacity to endure stress and shoulder burdens. Peaceful, happy, and very sensible, they know how to benefit themselves without depleting others. They have a great love of food and drink and do not worry much about their problems. Their ambitions are always reasonable, and they are able to find material success and security. Earth Boars are kind and thoughtful friends and reliable associates who seek tranquillity and domestic harmony in their lives.

INFLUENCE OF TIME OF BIRTH

The Hours of the Rat—11 P.M. to 1 A.M.

These are highly sociable Boars who are astute with money as well as in their assessments; they know how to cultivate beneficial relationships.

The Hours of the Ox—1 A.M. to 3 A.M.

Strong-tempered and opinionated Boars with precise habits; they are more in control of their sensual appetites.

The Hours of the Tiger—3 A.M. to 5 A.M.

Big-hearted, daring, athletic, and impulsive Boars who are guided by their emotions and are very open to the influence of others.

The Hours of the Rabbit—5 A.M. to 7 A.M.

These Boars are not nearly as obliging as they pretend to be and will not shoulder any more burdens than they have to, but are nonetheless easygoing and make great party animals.

The Hours of the Dragon—7 A.M. to 9 A.M.

Strong and dutiful, these Boars are devoted wholeheartedly to their loved ones. Both signs are direct, strong but innocent.

The Hours of the Snake—9 A.M. to 11 A.M.

These are stealthy and more secretive Boars with fewer scruples about taking what they want.

The Hours of the Horse—11 A.M. to 1 P.M.

These Boars are more selfish and inconsiderate, which actually serves to temper the Boar's excessive generosity and naiveté, making them able to more readily profit from their dealings with others.

The Hours of the Sheep—1 P.M. to 3 P.M.

Sentimental and compassionate, these Boars are easily duped. They will work hard for others and are overly generous.

The Hours of the Monkey—3 P.M. to 5 P.M.

These Boars are not easily tricked, as the Monkey protects them from the Boar's innocence and naiveté. Their friendly exterior conceals a calculating greed.

The Hours of the Rooster—5 P.M. to 7 P.M.

Well-intentioned but impractical, these Boars are quixotic and will take on tremendous tasks that reap little to no reward.

The Hours of the Dog—7 P.M. to 9 P.M.

These Boars have sound judgment and are less sensual and indulgent. They are intolerant of deceit and will be relentless in their revenge on those who lie to them.

The Hours of the Boar—9 P.M. to 11 P.M.

Honest, straightforward, loyal, sturdy, energetic, generous, and sensuous Boars.

THE BOAR'S PROSPECTS FOR COMING YEARS

The Year of the Boar—2007

Life will be stable and there will be some progress and gain, although Boars could experience conflict at work or at home.

There may be some chronic health problems. Winter brings new friends and opportunities.

The Year of the Rat—2008

A year of uncertainties, in which Boars are beset by worries that hinder their progress. Work and home life are unsettled, and there may be losses where Boars had expected gains.

The Year of the Ox—2009

A good year for business, in which prospects are readily apparent; gambles could pay off handsomely. There could be some romantic or family troubles or complications.

The Year of the Tiger—2010

Boars will encounter difficulties this year that they may have to face alone; they may be burdened by unexpected expenses such as fines, legal fees, or taxes.

The Year of the Rabbit—2011

There are some financial gains this year, and home life is peaceful and happy, with a considerable amount of socializing and entertaining.

The Year of the Dragon—2012

Boars will gain recognition, the respect of their associates, and the support of powerful people, but may face some health problems or the loss of some personal belongings.

The Year of the Snake—2013

A hectic, busy, and unsettling year, with moderate success. There will problems with the opposite sex and some sad news at home.

The Year of the Horse—2014

A good and prosperous year for family and career. Boars should avoid speculation or entrusting funds to others. Benefits formerly withheld become available.

The Year of the Sheep—2015

Finances are at a standstill, but there will gains this year in the form of knowledge, training, or career development.

The Year of the Monkey—2016

Although Boars may suffer financial losses and domestic and personal problems, they will be able to borrow money and find people who can help solve their problems.

The Year of the Rooster—2017

Boars must be patient with difficult and complex negotiations. Progress is hampered or interrupted, and obstacles require time and effort to overcome. Home life, however, remains calm and supportive.

Aspirations will be frustrated, as difficulties arise out of past errors or neglect. Boars must be careful about whom they rely on and be open to constructive criticism.

SOME FAMOUS BOARS

Woody Allen, Julie Andrews, Lucille Ball, Humphrey Bogart, Maria Callas, Al Capone, Chiang Kai-shek, Ernest Hemingway, Charlton Heston, Alfred Hitchcock, Hubert Humphrey, King Hussein, Andrew Jackson, Henry Kissinger, Lee Kuan Yew, Field Marshal Montgomery, Merle Oberon, Prince Rainier of Monaco, Claude Rains, Sir Terence Rattigan, Ronald Reagan, Françoise Sagan, Roy Schneider, Robert Taylor.

GENERAL OUTLOOK 2007–2020

Fire Dog: January 29, 2006 (+)

Fire Boar: February 18, 2007 (-)

Earth Rat: February 7, 2008 (+)

Earth Ox: January 26, 2009 (-)

Metal Tiger: February 10, 2010 (+)

Metal Hare/Rabbit: February 3, 2011 (-)

Water Dragon: January 23, 2012 (+)

Water Snake: February 10, 2013 (-)

Wood Horse: January 31, 2014 (+)

Wood Ram/Sheep: February 19, 2015 (-)

Fire Monkey: February 9, 2016 (+)

Fire Rooster: January 28, 2017 (-)

Earth Dog: February 16, 2018 (+)

Earth Boar: February 5, 2019 (-)

Metal Rat: January 25, 2020 (+)

The Year of the Rat is one of opportunity and good prospects. Business in general is forecast as being good. Anything that began in the year of the Rat should in theory be successful.

The Year of the Fire Rat—A year in which business is aggressive, dynamic, and competitive. A year marked by self-determination and the active pursuit of ideals.

The Year of the Wood Rat—An unconventional year in which we are inclined to be inquisitive, intuitive, apprehensive, adaptable, and motivated by diligence.

The Year of the Earth Rat—A year in which we seek permanence and stability. Our goals are more realistic although much is based on trust.

The Year of the Metal Rat—A very good year for money making ventures, characterized by careful thought and sensitivity but also in which greed, envy, and possessiveness can become manifest.

The Year of the Water Rat—A year in which traditional values such as education tend to be embraced.

The Year of the Ox—The sort of problems that are encountered in the year of the Ox tend to be home front problems that seem to be never ending. The Ox year needs discipline and it is not the time for unruly behavior or taking short cuts. In this year success is achieved solely through hard work.

The Year of the Fire Ox—A money-oriented year in which we are motivated by power and are prone to be combative, but in which dealings tend be open and honest.

The Year of the Wood Ox—A year marked by a return to traditional values and customs. The overall climate is more accommodating, ethical, fair-minded, and motivated by honesty.

The Year of the Earth Ox—A resolute year, marked by endurance, patience, focus, discipline, and a strong concern for the truly genuine.

The Year of the Metal Ox—A year of confrontation. People and dealings tend to be stubborn and intense, refusing to bend or compromise and motivated by both conceit and conviction.

The Year of the Water Ox—A systematic and practical year. Dealings are levelheaded, patient, and goal oriented.

The Year of the Tiger is a bold and volatile year in which everything is taken to its limit. It can also be a year of war, disasters, and all kinds of disputes. It is a year of massive change for better or for worse.

The Year the Fire Tiger—A volatile and dramatic year, marked by self-reliance, impulsiveness, generosity, and enthusiasm, but also erratic and unpredictable.

The Year of the Wood Tiger—Certainly a pioneering year, filled with enchantment, risk-taking, and adventurous schemes but motivated by co-operation and tolerance.

The Year of the Earth Tiger—A year in which we are hard working, impartial, and responsible. Great value is placed on academic studies and accomplishments and things of true and lasting worth.

The Year of the Metal Tiger—An aggressive year in which dealings in general tend to be driven more by self interest.

The Year of the Water Tiger—A more tranquil year. Dealings and perceptions are unbiased, open minded, and honest.

The Year of the Rabbit is in sharp contrast to the explosive year of the tiger. It is a year of placidity and respite; a carefree happy year that will be both temperate and relaxed.

The Year of the Fire Rabbit—A year in which the world in general seems more loving, unobtrusive, sensitive, perceptive, and motivated by refinement and aesthetic appreciation.

The Year of the Wood Rabbit—Dealings and attitudes tend to be more thoughtful, kindly, motivated by generosity, liberal and compassionate.

The Year of the Earth Rabbit—A solemn year marked by fairness, but also there is a tendency to be withdrawn, money-oriented, and motivated by appropriation.

The Year of the Metal Rabbit—A temperamental and crafty year. Dealings can be rational but covert, and there is a greater than usual attention to detail and nervous sensitivity.

The Year of the Water Rabbit—A quiet and somewhat introverted year, marked by a general empathy and a desire for peace.

The Year of the Dragon is one that brings happiness and good fortune. It is one of the most positive and strongest of all of the twelve star signs. During the year of the Dragon there will be violent acts of nature, with an electrifying ambience and things coming in waves. For those considering marriage or starting a new venture or business it is an favorable year.

The Year of the Fire Dragon—A year marked by challenge in which we also are driven by both compassion and aspiration.

The Year of the Wood Dragon—Both arrogance and inspiration are characteristic of this year, marked by frankness and openness in all dealings.

The Year of the Earth Dragon—A steady and leisurely year, but also marked by courage, practicality and an acute sense of law and authority.

The Year of the Metal Dragon—A year of contest and intense competition in which dealings and attitudes can tend to be resolute and inflexible.

The Year of the Water Dragon—A year in which we can tend to be more unrestrained, although attitudes are democratic and there is a general willingness to negotiate.

The Year of the Snake is a somewhat changeable year, filled with preparation, contemplation and much reflection. Often breakthroughs are made but achieved in secrecy or silence. Generally the Snake year is not a calm year, possibly a year of hard dealings, turmoil and even war if differences cannot be resolved. The year of the Snake is the most negative force of all of the signs.

The Year of the Fire Snake—A year in which dealings are motivated by authority and power. Actions and attitudes tend to be self-assured, masterful, but wary and unbending.

The Year of the Wood Snake—A year marked more by a sense of understanding, accord and consistency. Dealings will be discreet, serious, and at times mysterious and fascinating.

The Year of the Earth Snake—A year in which traditional values are embraced and upheld. People tend to be unrelenting and dependable.

The Year of the Metal Snake—A vigorous year, marked by scheming, caution, and a strong desire for material wealth.

The Year of the Water Snake—A money oriented year in which dealings are thoughtful, intuitively insightful, and patience is at a premium.

The Year of the Horse is a year of progress. It is a very happy-go-lucky, frantic, and wild year that is both adventurous and satisfying. There will be an upward trend to the year with a great deal of good humor. It is a year for going it alone, perhaps with some surprises in store but on the whole a courageous and daring year.

The Year of the Fire Horse—A highly strung, powerful, and capricious year, filled with adventures of all kinds, both amorous and otherwise. A year in which passions and desires can run high, and which dealings and actions are driven by will and desire.

The Year of the Wood Horse—A year of advancement and progress in which people tend to be helpful, dependable, and methodical although at times peculiar and idiosyncratic.

The Year of the Earth Horse—A slower year marked in general by reliability, rationality, and prudence.

The Year of the Metal Horse—A year of fruitful challenge. The climate tends to be egotistical and obstinate.

The Year of the Water Horse—A flexible although inconsistent year, marked by energetic although capricious or erratic action.

The Year of the Sheep is a time of gentle caring and the cultivation of creative talent, imagination and emotion. Harmony and moderation are the key words with a warning about the danger of negativity.

The Year of the Fire Sheep—A more aggressive, dramatic, and lively year. People are motivated by deed and action, and there can be a tendency for things to get competitive and even malicious.

The Wood Sheep—A year of trust and consideration. Actions tend to be motivated by loyalty, generosity, and sentimentality.

The Earth Sheep—A year of both anxiety and hope in which traditional values are embraced and people tend to act more autonomously.

The Metal Sheep—A year of unbalance in which people tend to feel defensive and vulnerable, although there is still a strong desire to seek accord in all things.

The Water Sheep—A gentle year often marked by unexpected opportunity.

The Year of the Monkey is one where anything and everything is possible, a year when things that appear impossible will succeed. With all of this success around no-one will know what they are doing. A haggling and scheming year full of luck in which no one will accept no for answer.

The Year of the Fire Monkey—A lively and creative year, filled with ambition, covetousness and rivalry.

The Year of the Wood Monkey—A more cautious although restless year, one filled with much talk and negotiation.

The Year of the Earth Monkey—A more sober and sullen year, as Monkey years go. The general atmosphere is one of curiosity coupled with practical intent.

The Year of the Metal Monkey—Things tend to be more consistent and reliable. A year of self-reliance and enterprise, in which we tend to be more fashion-conscious and stylish.

The Year of the Water Monkey—A year of collaboration and driving ambition. Dealings can be marked by a certain degree elusiveness and clever trickery, with each party scheming to out maneuver the other.

The Year of the Rooster is one of a huge dissipation of energy and precarious balance which can often lead to arguments. It is a cautious year where no one wants to listen to anyone else, resulting in frequent disagreements and frayed nerves. However no one will undergo too much hardship.

The Year of the Fire Rooster—An unpredictable and argumentative year marked by hard work and strict adherence to principles.

The Year of the Wood Rooster—A year marked by dependability and disciplined and selfless acts in our dealings with others.

The Year of the Earth Rooster—A year in which things seem well-organized and efficient, in which great attention is paid to both mundane and intricate details.

The Year of the Metal Rooster—A year of hard work and practical opportunities but one in which we are motivated by idealistic concerns.

The Year of the Water Rooster—A lively and inventive year, marked by practical ingenuity.

The Year of the Dog is a year for reflection and to assess one's values. There will be disturbances and revolts, but as the Dog is always on the lookout, honesty will always rule the day. This year will see great benevolent and idealistic deeds and various unusual changes; a time when broadmindedness and fairness will be supported. Although this year is one of great cynicism a sense of balance and tranquility will be upheld.

The Year of the Fire Dog—Definitely a dramatic year in which people tend to be ferocious, alluring, self-assertive, and passionate. There can be many obstacles to overcome, as the dog is circumspect and on guard and perhaps overly diligent as watcher at the gate.

The Year of the Wood Dog—A year often characterized by adaptability, generosity, logic, and reason.

The Year of the Earth Dog—A year of caution and wariness, but one marked by a strong awareness of morality and fairness.

The Year of the Metal Dog—A year greatly feared by the Tibetans, who see it as a time of strife, calamity, and upheaval. A year where people tend to rigidly stand their ground, but also marked by the dog's generosity and judiciousness.

The **Year of the Water Dog**—A more laid-back year in which we tend to be more self-indulgent and philosophical.

THE YEAR OF THE BOAR

The Year of the Boar is of benevolence and abundance and a good year for business. Life in this year will be lived to the full and although there will be uncertainty it will be minimal. It is a rich year with impetuous acts, but care is recommended with any matters concerning money. The Boar is the symbol for great courage and integrity.

The Year of the Fire Boar—A year where our actions are often motivated by affection. There is an overall tendency to be stubborn, sensual, and irresponsible.

The Year of the Wood Boar—A year in which people can tend to be more deceitful and scheming, shrewd and ambitiousness. There will be many manipulations for personal gain, but it is also a good for business deals and financial ventures.

The Year of the Earth Boar—A calm but industrious year. The atmosphere is friendly and welcoming, but filled with common sense and more a practical and mundane view of the world.

The Year of the Metal Boar—A lively and extroverted year, marked by fortitude and patience. A year in which we will not accept defeat without first putting up a good fight.

The Year of the Water Boar—A gregarious year of peace and diplomacy, marked by much adroitness in bargaining with opponents and arriving at peaceful settlements.

TO LEARN MORE

Following are some good resources if you want to go further in your knowledge:

Paul Carus. *Chinese Astrology*. La Salle, IL: Open Court, 1974.

E. A. Crawford and Teresa Kennedy. *Chinese Elemental Astrology*. New York: Signet, 1990.

Paula Delsol. *Chinese Astrology*. New York: Hipporene Books, 1972.

Jean Michel Huon de Kermadec. *The Way of Chinese Astrology: The Four Pillars of Destiny*. London: Unwin, 1983.

Man-Ho Kowk. *Chinese Astrology: Forecast Your Future from Your Chinese Horoscope*. Boston: C. E. Tuttle, 1997.

Lau Kwok. *Secrets of Chinese Astrology: A Handbook for Self-Discovery*. New York: Tongu Books, 1994.

T. C. Lai. *Animals of the Chinese Zodiac*. Hong Kong: Hong Kong Book Center, 1979.

Theodora Lau. *The Chinese Horoscopes' Guide to Relationships: Love and Marriage, Friendship and Business*. New York: Main Street Books, 1997.

ABOUT THE AUTHOR

Damian Sharp, an Asian studies scholar, was born in Australia and currently resides in San Francisco, California. The author of *Simple Feng Shui*, he is the recipient of two Literary Fellowship Awards from the Australian Council for the Arts. His collection of short stories, *When a Monkey Speaks,* was published in 1994. Mr. Sharp adapted the title story of the collection for a screenplay which is in development for a motion picture. His short stories have appeared in the *Chicago Review* and the *Denver Quarterly,* and he has written for *Soho Weekly News, Rice Magazine,* and *California Magazine.*

TO OUR READERS

Conari Press, an imprint of Red Wheel/Weiser, publishes books on topics ranging from spirituality, personal growth, and relationships to women's issues, parenting, and social issues. Our mission is to publish quality books that will make a difference in people's lives—how we feel about ourselves and how we relate to one another. We value integrity, compassion, and receptivity, both in the books we publish and in the way we do business.

Our readers are our most important resource, and we value your input, suggestions, and ideas about what you would like to see published. Please feel free to contact us, to request our latest book catalog, or to be added to our mailing list.

Conari Press
An imprint of Red Wheel/Weiser, LLC
500 Third Street, Suite 230
San Francisco, CA 94107
www.redwheelweiser.com